Get Yourself on TV
& What to Do When You Get There

JAN FOX

Get Yourself on TV & What to Do When You Get There

Copyright © 2013 by T.O.Press. All rights reserved. Printed in the United States of America.

No part of this book may be used or reproduced in any manner whatsoever without written permission except in the case of brief quotations embodied in critical articles and reviews.

For information:
Fox Talks at www.foxtalks.com or info@foxtalks.com.
Fox Talks LLC

ISBN 978-0-578-09798-5

Book Design By Dylan Halpern.

Dedication

To the memory of my Pop - Tom Fox, the rip roarin' street preacher, who taught me to lick my lips and smile at the audience. That was while playing an accordion and singing on street corners, in nursing home, jails, old churches – anywhere he could find somebody to listen. Try not to picture that accordion part.

The man had the purest heart. Tom Fox's rattle trap house was the "House of Favors" on the corner of Montgomery and Locust Streets in lovely downtown Shelbyville, IN. You needed something. Tom Fox found a way to give it.

To my daughter - Kristin Nash Michalak, Tom Fox reincarnated, except for the rip-roarin' preacher part. Full of exuberance, adventure, no fear. Loyal to the bone. A great speaker, motivator, and sales person. She wins you over. She has been my teacher!

To my hubby – Michael Anthony O'Sullivan, simply the rock. THE ONE for me!

Contents

The Door to the Studio	1
You – The Research Assistant	9
You – The Producer	21
You – The Delivery Man	33
You – The Bundle of Nerves	43
You – The Determinator	57
You – The Stylist	75
You – The Prep Fanatic	83
You – The Performance Consultant	87
You – The Perfect Guest	105
You – The Host Tamer	113
Fox Talks Extras	131
About The Author....	153
Image Credits	157

Acknowledgements

My husband, Sully, thinks a computer grows out of my lap every night. Thanks to this very special man who never complains about a wife who never stops.

To all my friends who think I must have forgotten them while I cranked this book out: we'll do coffee, play golf, and talk soon.

To every person, non-profit group, community activist who ever brought me a good news story, I thank you from the bottom of my heart. Those stories from Big Brothers – Big Sisters, JDRF, American Cancer Society Women's Golf Tournaments, Habitat for Humanity, Busy Bees in Southeast DC, UNCF, Children's Hospital Center, countless heroes, and many others helped soothe my horrible ache after witnessing many murder victims, devastated families, fires, fatal car accidents, and cases of abused children. I needed your stories to give our viewers and me hope for our world.

To countless small businesses and entrepreneurs: I hope our stories about you helped you grow. You made my Friday Finds some of the most fun segments I did – the apple orchard that let families rent a tree to take care of and help preserve the farm, the jewelry shop that fixed watches at the cheapest price, the haunted forest put on for kids by college students, the circus school (Leonardo the Grip really caught me, as I flew through the air on a Trapeze!), the gondola builder on the South River, the hair repair lady, the chef with 5 squash recipes, and on and on and on.

After speaking for 30 years to thousands of people, I accidentally ran into the National Speakers Association. That group set me on a path to sharing my stories and experiences in a more organized, business-like fashion.

You know who you are - my supporters and mentors:

Ron Culberson – the first person I ever met with to talk to about NSA and speaking. You made me laugh big time. When I told you I believed in "tweaks", you told me to quickly buy URLS. Thanks for the faith!

Bill Cates – a master mind that works in systems and programs with great discipline. I need more of that! You made me answer the tough questions about this business. I owe you.

Sam Horn – a wordsmith of the highest order. You also gave me the confidence to believe that someone would really listen, if I spoke!

Willie Jolley – you remembered me!! Thanks for selling me your speaker kit. It was my first investment!

Max Dixon – you sharpened my stories, and you made me stand up straight when I speak!

Kim Roman Corle and Colin Dunn – my buddies who sat with me at our very first NSA DC meeting. Anything I do that might matter, they helped me shape.

Michael Sands, Mike Schmidtmann, Liz Fletcher-Brown, Josef Martens, Susan Kousek, Sally Strackbein,

Simon T. Bailey, Ed Robinson, David Newman, you have given me guidance on many fronts.

Chela Hardy, my Virtual Assistant – thanks for every piece you picked up, every stray detail you put in place, and every path you paved for this rookie business woman.

Amy Sievers !!! This incredibly talented woman jumped through hoops to get the Foxtalks.com website up, format books, design collateral, and corral me into some sense of business order.

Dylan Halpern, you know you saved me with deadlines trying to re-format this book! Thanks so very much! I'm grateful you fell in my path.

You are all amazing!!

As my Pop would say, many blessings to all of you.

Foreword

This book? It is just a compilation of all the answers I have given over the years to those who asked me how to get a story idea on TV.

You made me write this little book – every last one of you who ever asked me my most often asked question: "How do I get my idea on TV?", and the second most often asked question: "What do I do when I get there?"

If this plain talk, no-nonsense, how-to book helps one survivor, one healer, one do-gooder, one helper, one idea generator, one kid mentor land even a 4 minute TV segment, it will have been worth it.

We need all of you. We need your message. We need your courage to tell us your story. If you land the segment, send me a note. Tell me what it was and how you did it. You may force me to write Book 2: Great Ideas that Made it to TV.

Another book is forthcoming about the Power of Tweaks: *MICROacts to MAXimize Potential*. Ahead of time, I thank anybody who helped me clarify my message: Think Big. ACT small. Think Near-sighted, then Farsighted. Let the action begin! Enjoy the results!

Part One

The Door to the Studio

No Fax, No Phone, No Email, No Books

FAX: Now a thing of the dark ages.

PHONE: Click! Your voice mail is deleted.

EMAIL: One of hundreds that TV producers and reporters get every day.

BOOKS: Go in a box under the producer's desk. The staff goes through them from time to time to find a free gift for someone they know.

NO RESPONSE

None of these will get you the response you want from a TV station – even if the story or the segment you are pitching is a good one.

Press Release Release

- **OLD TIME PRESS RELEASES DON'T GRAB ATTENTION ANYMORE.** Never use white paper and black ink. Bright, brighter, brightest with ribbons or trinkets or food attached work much better.
- **NEVER EVER EVER WRITE IN PARAGRAPHS.** Use bullets and just the basics: who, what, why, where, when, HOW.
- **START WITH THE SOLUTION AT THE TOP:** Lose 5 Pounds Fast. Learn Linkedin in 5 Minutes. Kids Clean Your Streets FREE.
- **LOAD UP WITH LOOT:** Include something that makes you memorable.

Even with all of this attention you give to your press release, it probably will be one of 100s or even 1000s that get to the newsroom every day. It won't get a producer's attention. Why?

No Good News

Local TV stations used to be the easiest place to start, if you wanted to pitch a good news story, or a segment about a book, or a concept guaranteed to change the viewers' lives. No more. Locals are now reduced to VERY local news, if they want to survive. Murders. Robberies. Car crashes. Weather. Local sports.

You and I get our national news and happy or informational segments from cable stations and the internet. Most local talk shows and info-tainment programs have bitten the proverbial new age TV dust. It was about the money.

It sounds like a long shot that you might get on TV, doesn't it? It is, but be patient. We'll get to specific actions in a few pages, but first, a little preparation.

The "Know Somebody" Door

So what do you do? It's true. Knowing somebody is the easiest way to get your idea on a TV segment.

A singing quartet – The Doo Wop Cops – made it to air because I met them at a golf tournament and told my week-end producer about them.

A group of line dancers ended up on the morning show because they hooked up with a favorite charity.

A man who wrote a not-so-famous kids' book got a 2 minute segment, because he was once the subject of a golf club collecting story. He called the producer again and got on.

Could you possibly have even a remote connection to anyone in that TV station? That's your first point of contact.

6 Degrees Of Separation

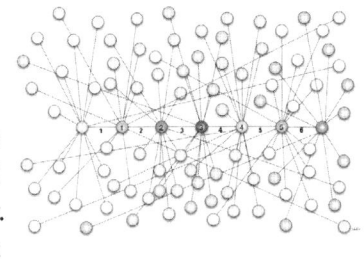

If you don't know someone personally, think about all the people you do know. Who, in your circles, is most likely to play tennis or share car pool duties with a producer or an underling at the assignment desk? Which of your friends is involved in charities where TV celebrities served as host or emcee?

Who has mentioned someone they know at a station, in your past? Think hard. The "know somebody" even "in passing" door is easier than starting from scratch.

No Excuses, Linkedin!

If you log onto Linkedin right now, you can search "Producer" and end up with 1,530 names!

If you search "Groups", you'll find 141 TV Producers Groups! Some with as many as 25,000+ members.

Pick your city. Look for your local news producers. You will find names of actual people you can contact any number of ways. Social Media has made it so much easier to find TV people who can help you.

Willie's Law of Talk

Ask all the people you know if they know anybody and talk to everybody about the good idea you have for a segment.

World famous speaker, Willie Jolley, says to talk to people in the grocery store about what you do and what you know! Talk to anybody who will listen.

After I heard his CD, with his talk it up admonition, I told some women at a New Year's Eve party that I was now speaking and coaching on a more regular basis. I mentioned the name of my company, Fox Talks, and that started a whole group conversation about what I do. I jokingly said, "I just talk, and I teach people to talk better".

That led to the next question: How did I come up with the name?

My answer: I went to a high-priced brander to come up with a company plan and a brand. I came away with a plan, but not a good name. I did the usual. I whined about it to my hubby. He said, "Why don't you just call it Fox Talks, because you certainly do!"

That did it. After the laughter subsided, One of the women, a partner in a law firm invited me to do a presentation for her associates – for a handsome fee!

Ok, she wasn't a TV producer, but if that can happen the first time I mention a new company, think how many times it can help you meet a producer, if you talk about it everywhere you go.

The more I talk to people about my new speaking business, the more speaking engagements and coaching clients, I get. The more you talk about how your idea is made for TV, the closer to a producer you get.

Your spouse may not appreciate this advice, but KEEP TALKING!!

Willie's Law of Talk works!

Somebody you know will know a producer!

Part Two

You – The Research Assistant

You as Researcher

If no luck with finding a connection, find out who does consumer or health stories on the channels you watch. Who covers retirement or the environment? Who focuses on moms or schools? That is all such easy information to get, by simply watching or by combing the station's website.

It's so cool these days for people to say, "Oh, I don't watch much TV." Or "I hate local news. It's so gory." It's not cool to be one of those naysayers if you want to *GET YOURSELF ON TV!* You have to commit to watching all of your local stations. Get over yourself, sit in the easy chair, and simply watch.

Listen very carefully to what local TV reporters and anchors talk about on their shows. They are giving you constant clues as to what they want and need for their programs. Can you become a solution with a few tweaks to your topic?

The Fit

Can what you do be re-purposed or re-packaged to fit one of their topics? Listen for hints about what they like or might be interested in outside of their TV jobs. I know who talks about fancy shoes on a noon show, and who plays in charity tennis matches, and which anchor had a heart attack and wrote a book about it. You are looking for a "fit" for your topic.

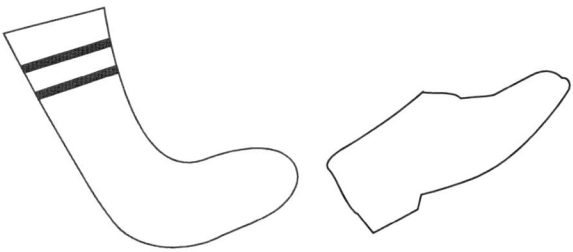

Keep notes as you hear what they mention in transition chatter. That's when one anchor says, "And now let's go over to John with sports. I saw you out there hitting the tennis ball earlier." These "throws" to one another are their cues to start talking for their segment. It happens when the anchor tosses to the Health or Consumer reporter or to a street reporter on the scene. Did you hear a "fit" for your story?

A local reporter does a segment every week about a child who needs to be adopted. Dr. Chris Efessiou is the author of a clever book, *Chief Daddy Officer*. He is the CEO of a pharmaceutical company. The book is about how he used business principles to raise his own daughter by himself. At age 7, she came to live with him.

Suddenly, for teaching her how to make the bed, he needed to use "Gap Analysis". Of course, he needed a "Strategic Plan" and "Budget Adjustment" from the very beginning. And every parent of a teenager needs to know about "Trust and Verify". The book is funny, but also very touching. The letter from his daughter on her wedding day will make you teary!

When I started to suggest cookies to get that reporter's attention, immediately, in his slight accent, Chris said, "I don't do cookies!"

Not deterred, I described a cookie in the shape of a little girl, another in the shape of a dollar sign, a necktie, and a book.

We then created an opening line to a note to include in a cookie bouquet:

"What do these cookies have in common? They tell the story of a dad (necktie) who used business principles (dollar sign) to raise his daughter (little girl) by himself. Included in this basket is the book I wrote to tell my story…"

His wife asked me if she should have the basket delivered or deliver it herself. Legitimate question, but I asked her if she would rather have the courier or herself have a potential conversation with the reporter or producer. She hand delivered the basket to the local station.

She asked for the reporter by name. Who should come out to receive it? The reporter herself! YES! She invited Chris to come do an interview! YES! The week before Father's Day. A similar basket got him to do interviews at two other stations!

Chris had two perfect "fits" with the station: 1. It was Father's Day. 2. He knew which reporter dealt with kids' issues.

Can you find your "fit" with local reports or anchors?

Clock Watcher

Watch around the clock for a few days. Where in local news do you see the most repeats of stories you saw earlier? Where does the content seem to drag? Where does the weatherman get a second or third hit in a half hour show?

Hint: Weekends and mid-morning shows. Because of budget cuts, weekends get skeleton crews - sometimes just one or, at most, two photographers and one editor to fill a 30 minute show. Some local stations are just using their early morning anchors to do another show at 9 or 10AM, instead of buying expensive programming.

These shows aren't ratings grabbers, but they need content. You have a better chance of getting on at these times. If you make it, that means you get a link to the segment with a network logo on it, and a line or two about your experience to post on your website.

A young activist, Omekongo Dibinga, watched the clock. He has been invited to many nations around the world to speak at youth rallies. He is amazing. He is calling on 1,000,000 kids from around the globe to sign a com-

mitment to be an *UP-STANDER*, the title of his moving book.

Omekongo has this incredible ability to tell stories with new age poetry and a hip hop-like beat. He knew that a local network noon anchor hosted a segment called, "Heroes."

He put his CDs and his *UPSTANDER* book in a

box, with a laminated sheet laying out his entire segment. He knew the anchor woman liked chocolate, so he added six red velvet cupcakes to his box. YES! He got booked for an interview. Better yet, the producer said she loved his segment and will look for other ways to use him!!!

He watched the news, watched the clock, found his niche, used his "fit."

Calendar Watcher

Getting invited to do a segment may not happen when you want it. Your job is to figure out when the TV station *needs* it.

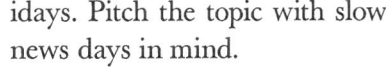

Watch your calendar. If you see holidays or government days off, you know the news desk is looking to MAKE action. Plan ahead. See if any of your topics fit the holidays. Pitch the topic with slow news days in mind.

Dawn Peters, the lovely Mind & Body ShapeShifter pictured on the front of this book, sent out an email blast to her list: *How to Eat, Drink, and Still Shrink at the Holidays.* I'm on her list, so I received it.

I loved the title, so I shot a reply telling her this was a perfect segment for the morning show at a local network station. I sent a quick email to a producer I knew. She was interested.

I told Dawn to send a basket of goodies – everything anyone could eat at the holidays and still shrink. She hand delivered it to the station with a Ready-Made Segment attached.

Within minutes of the delivery, Dawn got the call. The producer invited her in to tape a couple of segments that would air before the holidays, saying, "That was the most organized segment I ever saw- in a basket!"

Dawn did a great job on the set and was invited back to do another segment that is calendar related– Get Beach Body Ready! I watched it and she was great! Of course, she is invited back – again!

What segments can you pitch that fit around the holidays?

Web Window

As I've mentioned, most TV personalities are writing blogs and posting web content. Many have separate web sites. All of them can be found under TEAM or some such tab on their station's website.

Below are some blogs I know and sometimes follow in Washington, DC. I give them to you as examples of what you may find in your neighborhood. These names may change or move to another station, or the station may get a new News Director and switch their assignments. You will get the idea just the same.

WUSA TV'S Peggy Fox: MomsLikeMe.com where Metro DC moms meet. She covers all kinds of great stories about kids and what parents can do with them. Can you stretch your topic to fit that category?

JC Hayward: Welcome to a FaceBook Page about DVM Our Time WUSA 9 News. Join FaceBook to start connecting with DVM Our Time WUSA 9 News. This site is all about retirees:

- All important benefit and regulations items
- Many tips on what to do with all of your new spare time
- Lots of postings about groups that meet on many topics of interest
- Information and tips on saving and spending in retirement

Rebecca Cooper is the host of Washington Business Report on the ABC station. Her weekly guests include: local consultants, coaches, CEOs, and other business leaders who share their topics of interest for small businesses and entrepreneurs.

What could you offer to that show? Most business topics are worn by now, but the trick is to find a new angle, or report new results, or announce a new book.

Rebecca also has a great blog for Business and Finance. Start posting. Post with your theme without sounding salesy. Offer tips and creative content, not sales pitches.

Another reporter has a blog about, **"Sex and Gender in the Workplace"**. No more comment on that one, but maybe good for Life Coaches, Therapists, Relationship Coaches, Government specialists on the topic, and Diversity specialists, to name a few.

You will find interesting blogs and many more like these at stations all across the country. Peruse these sites in your city. Post comments. Post again. Get to know the writers. Don't be bashful. Subtly suggest segments that you could do on their television shows. Make sure you stay on their point, or they won't read your posts after that.

Staying in balance, stretch your topic to find hooks for your stories. The health reporter is doing a series on cancer survivors. You are one, or you work with cancer survivors. That's your invitation right away. Just be sure to propose a specific angle. They don't like generic proposals that they have to work to refine. More on this later.

The sports reporter does stories about local sports related heroes. You coach the local Special Olympics team. You get the idea.

Notes:

Part Three

You – The Producer

Your Ready-Made Segment in a Box, Basket, or Bag

I've mentioned baskets and boxes. Here's why. Even direct mailing companies know to send "lumpy" mail.

They stick an object in the envelope to entice you to open it. You always open the mail that comes in a colorful tube, don't you?

When you send an email or leave a message in the newsroom, they generate zero buzz or sizzle, but if you send or deliver your segment in a box or basket or even a bag, think about it. Somebody has to come out to the reception desk, pick it up, and walk it back to the newsroom or production department.

Imagine what happens when somebody walks into one of those areas with that box, basket, or bag: people stand up, walk toward it, or, at least, holler all across the newsroom.

"Hey, what's in the box?"

"Whadga get?"

"Anything to eat in that?"

I promise. I have witnessed that onslaught personally many, many times.

I always use a twist on the old cliché:

"You have to think INside the BOX to get Inside the TV Studio."

The Eyeballs Have It

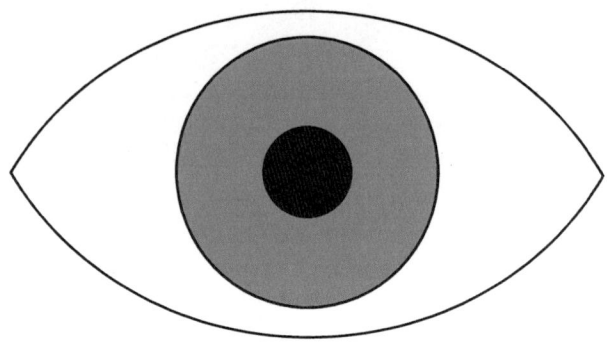

Start thinking out your eyeballs!

You must think about your story or segment visually. Story pitchers spend most of their time thinking about content, and then wordsmithing it to death, literally. They send numerous pages describing a story with little or no visual support.

So many pitchers and authors still view TV as talk radio. They worry about the words and the message and forget that the message gets imagined better by producers, if they get visuals.

Producers don't have time to read. They need visual aids! Word stories or pitches, no matter how good, don't even make it to the editing room, let alone on the editing room floor.

What props or photos or videos or stunts can you bring that will make the story memorable – visually?

The big question in your mind the whole time you are working on your segment that you are proposing is: What will your viewers see? With TV, the viewers remember what they SEE, not what they hear.

At the very least, develop slides your producer can run as you talk. Be sure to follow these Fox Talks PowerPoint Points

PowerPoint Points

AIRPLANE: Each slide needs a take-off, a flight, and a landing. Lead to the point, make the point, and then transition on to the next slide.

STORIES: Make each slide tell a part of the story, using words, graphs, and pictures. You fill in the gaps, engaging the audience in the story. Audiences relate to stories more than facts.

SPEED: Click to a new slide every 20-30 seconds. New media (web, social, mobile) are all about fast visuals, and that's what audiences expect. Keep it moving, unless in discussion.

UNDERSTANDING: Ask yourself, "How long does it take you to get the point of a slide?" If more than 10-15 seconds, the audience will lose interest and start texting under the table.

TO THE POINT: Use many more slides than you think will be necessary. Keep each slide simple. Talk shorter on each one. Three quick slides are more effective than one long slide.

SMALL WORDS: Never use full sentences or periods. Instead, use one and two syllable words in fragments. Statements work best in ONE line; only go to two if necessary.

BIG FONT: Use size 28 font and above. Smaller fonts can't be read easily after a few rows back. (If you need to put 'fine print' at the bottom as a source of data, use size 18).

SIMPLE FONT: Always use sans serif font. No little "feet" on the letters. Tahoma, Calibri, Verdana, Eras Demi, and Arial Rounded MT Bold, are good choices. Don't use plain Arial.

PICTURES: Think in pictures. Most words can be "said" in pictures, except for technical terms. Be careful, though, not to make images blurry or warped when changing their size.

IMAGE PLACEMENT: Move them around. Left side on one slide, right side on the next. Make the next photo the whole slide (but only if it doesn't blur).

GRAPHS: Got data to present? Put it in a graph. Better yet, enlarge the graph so that it takes up the entire screen.

REAL ESTATE: Use all the real estate on a slide for an important point. They don't need to see a title on every page, particularly if you are bringing the audience to a crescendo.

ANIMATION: Use animation sparingly, if at all. Use only fast fade ins and outs. You don't want to distract them wondering how you did that and then miss the point of the slide.

CONSISTENCY #1 : Changing fonts/colors can make a presentation more exciting, but if done without a design-eye, they can become distracting and look sloppy. Best to stick with a common font and color theme, adjusting sparingly to make a point.

CONSISTENCY #2: Vary the font size to emphasize copy, not JUST to change it for change sake. Use bolding and colors to make copy stand out.

CONSISTENCY #3: Use italics for quotes or to show fast action. Use straight up for name of person giving the quote.

PREPARATION: A PowerPoint is an aid to your presentation; it is NOT your presentation. Don't read it, present it. Time invested in preparation will substantially improve the result.

WIIFM?: Does every slide answer this for the audience? Make sure each slide has added value to the participants. Does it show an idea for increasing the ROI, wooing more clients, improving the participants' skillset?

KNOWABILITY & LIKABILITY: These may not be real words, but they are real factors that audiences use to tune in or out to your presentation. Each slide should represent who YOU are – how you think, speak, and act. The participant needs to identify with you on every slide.

SEEK HELP: Getting images placed correctly, fonts cleaned up, spacing right, etc. takes some work. You may not be an expert. Ask!

Your Personal Persuade the Producer Plan

To recap all of this information, simply use this Fox Talks Personal Persuade the Producer Plan to *GET YOURSELF ON TV.* Be sure to answer all the questions and do all the steps. Then you will be ready to go.

Start with your segment content preparation.

1. What do you speak about?
2. What would listeners SEE in their minds as you speak?
3. Can you change the normal title to a catchy visual image?
4. What are the most powerful images you present in your speech?
5. For TV, what would it take to make those images the very meat of your interview?
6. What Props could you bring to illustrate your points?
7. What demonstration could you do?
8. List the photos or print screens you could send to have pre-produced before you arrive for your segment?
9. Can you video some of your clients or some subjects that your producer could run during your interview?
10. List graphics you could design to explain your concepts.
11. If you have a book, can you take out all the set up, all the non-visual language, and pick a story to illustrate each point?
12. Can you tell each story in a humorous or moving manner in 4-5 sentences?

– What happened?
– What was the turning point?
– What was your lightbulb moment?
– What was the resolution?
– Why does it matter to the viewer?

Ready-Made Segment Plan

1. Look over all your prepared segment possibilities.
2. What do you have in the list that would make a great gift to send to the station?
3. Do the research to find a contact at the station – an anchor, a reporter, a manager name from the website. Name & Station address.
4. Hand deliver a box, bag, or other container with a related surprise or a basket of goodies, wine, flowers, or props that will have a direct connection to your segment.
5. Add a colorful LAMINATED sheet with:

    – very catchy title
    – your suggested segment introduction
    – list of 7 questions the interviewer can ask
    – an outro – what the interviewer can say at the end of your segment
    – your contact info
    – of course, a possible follow-up topic for your next segment.

6. Devise a follow-up plan. It can include a second product to drop off at the station or to have delivered. What would be that connection to your segment?
7. Talk up the receptionist at the lobby. Find out the name of the anchor's or reporter's producer.
8. Send a preview clue to the producer.

EXAMPLE:
Several years ago, I received as small invitation-type white envelope with my name handwritten on it.

When I opened it a little piece of red yarn fell out. Inside, it just said something like, "Stay tuned."

A week later, I received a small box with the cutest little, fluffy stuffed white kitty. Nothing else.

A week later, I received a ticket to the CATS opening in NYC, instructions on where to catch a bus from Boston to NYC. I would be joining other TV reporters on the trip.

NOW THAT WAS A PREVIEW PLAN, and I must say, one of my reporter days' highlights.

9. If you think of ANYTHING outside the scope of this plan, TRY it!!
10. If you can't think of anything you can do, enlist your most creative friends to brainstorm with you!!
11. **Don't think a publicist can do this for you.** Most of them send emails, your book, or an outdated press kit – UNLESS the publicist has personal relationships or connections with TV producers/managers. Find that out up front before you pay big money.

Bottom line:

How can you turn your content into moving action or pictures?

That's what producers want, because they know that's what viewers want. They see the past ratings. They can see where viewers clicked off, and almost always it will be at a talking head, boring segment. Top management rates the producers on how active and engaging their shows are.

They will welcome your help!

Part Four

You – The Delivery Man

Sealed and Ready for Special Delivery

A local Armenian Church sends a huge platter of homemade baklava and other treats to the weatherman every year.

And every year, he shows it on TV and announces that the festival is on.

NOTE: Newsrooms are notoriously hungry. The way to get on TV is often through the belly!

Coming up are several examples of segments that made it on TV, plus other potential ideas. As you read through them, keep your segment in mind. Start extrapolating from each one something you can use for your segment pitch.

Waaaaay Outside the Box

A Maryland woman started a recycle challenge to see which kids could pick up the most scrap metal from around their blocks. They enlisted a local artist they dubbed, "Recycle Man". He would turn all of the scrap into some cool sculpture at the end of the event. This is visual!

No amount of calling TV stations got a response. The organizer called someone she knew in the TV business to lobby for her. Still no luck.

So her reporter friend told her to put a box of scrap metal together. Make that a pretty box. Drop it off at the station with a note to the environmental reporter saying that you found it all on her street! Ask if she would like to meet some kids who are doing something about street junk.

She didn't have to go that whole route, but it's an example of a great idea to get attention.

The reporter friend got the segment on by begging the weekend assignment editor to let the photographer stop by to shoot a little video on his way back to the station with the Page 1 News story.

Yes! She got a follow-up story when the artist finished his sculpture. Both stories ran in other shows. The local organizer ended up on a national show and organized several other communities to become committed junk collectors.

Layout for an Injured Swimmer

Another community raised thousands of dollars for a local swimmer who was injured so severely that he was confined to a wheel chair, probably for life. One of the organizers, who knew me through someone else, called me.

I laid out the story for the health reporter: photos and home movies of the swimmer at his peak, still photos, an interview with the family talking about their difficulties, the swimmer taking the TV crew on a tour of his house with many modifications for his wheel chair, an interview with the organizer.

The Health Reporter could envision the swimmer and his family coming to the community meeting to pick up a big check. You can SEE each of these settings in your mind's eye, can't you? You have to create vivid pictures for a producer.

Invite the health reporter to emcee the event! The story made air on the weekends and again on a morning show.

Crab Savers

You want to do a story about Cleaning up the Bay Day? Drop off a box of hot steamed crabs with a note asking, "Do you like these succulent goodies? If you do, bring your cameras to watch local kids saving your Bay."

Better yet – leave the crabs kicking in the box with a recipe and Old Bay seasoning. You've just opened ALL the producer eyeballs in the newsroom with that box!

My own Seafood on TV Story

When I came to DC in 1990, to interview for a reporter job, the management offered me the position and said they would get back to me.

You know that nothing happened! This was the biggest moment in my career and I heard nothing for two weeks. The moving van was booked, but did I have a job? I left a couple of messages with the newsroom secretary, (before email) but feared being a nag.

One day, I was walking down a street in Portland, ME, and I saw a sign that said, "Will ship anywhere in 24 hours." I went in and bought two LIVE lobsters, put them in a box with a note to the news director that said, "It would be tough for me to leave these bad boys behind, but for you I would! I want your job!"

Within two days, the call came and the contract arrived shortly after. . I lasted 20 years!

You would kiss a lobster, too!

No Snag Social Media Segment

Social Media is a hot topic. The trouble with it on TV is that it takes too much time to flip from one page to another on your computer, if you are trying to do it live.

Make it different and fast paced. Put together a set of graphics using the anchor's FaceBook page. Call yourself the TV SAVVY NO SNAG SOCIAL MEDIA GURU, or some such thing.

Make a flip booklet of the pages you would show already packaged in a video. Just have the producer run the video as you talk. Even a slide show of print screens would help. Convince the producer you could make the segment fly by without the usual technical hitches that make those segments so boring.

BE SURE TO SHOW RESULTS! These segments also make the viewers lose interest because because they are just info that people can get anywhere else. Make yours different by showing photos of entrepreneurs or small businesses and tell 3-4 line stories:

- Jane Smith started following lots of her potential clients on Twitter. She agreed to increase the number of people she followed by 1000 in 30 days. At the end of the next 30 days, she had 3 new lucrative clients from those followers. That's worth 5 minutes a day!!
- John Jones hated Face Book, thought it was just for kids. His assistant made a commitment to post tips and good content every day. She reconnected with 2 of his former clients, equaling fast money in the bank with little work.

You can snap photos of people like these on the job or show them thanking a new client. We need to SEE the results!

Retirement Book Hook

"Leaving the cookies with the receptionist may get you in the door."

Say your book is book is about active retirees. Shoot your own highest quality video.

Put together a cookie bouquet with the cookies in the shapes of bicycles, golf balls, a dancer, and swimmer – the kinds of hobbies for active seniors. Add the video to the bouquet.

Have 6 articulate retirees, dressed to the 9s, show up in the lobby of a TV station about 5 minutes after a show has just finished. If you don't see the anchor come through the door, a small chatty group of younger people coming out might be the production/direction team. Ask if they will deliver the bouquet, the video, and some still photos to the retirement reporter. If not, leaving the cookies with the receptionist may still get you in the door.

Other Book Hooks

A great new book is, *Don't Let 'em Treat You Like a Girl*, by Liz Weber. How can that be turned into a visual story? Slides with examples or cartoons? Quick mini-movies- 30 seconds of women on the job giving the tips that are in the book. That would set up the tips for the interviewer and author to discuss.

Eileen Kugler has a new book on Diverse Schools. She could offer a couple of teens to go on TV with her in a segment about how they deal with their diverse school. It's still talking but from the most interesting perspectives. Of course, photos of the kids at school can show them in their setting – even more appealing!

Sam Horn's book, Tongue-Fu, is about getting along with difficult people. Maybe collect some photos or cartoon examples of difficult people. Make mini-movies of arguments between two people. Sam and the host could then unravel and analyze them. Maybe they could play them again the way that shows a win-win for both parties.

These are just 3 examples of ways to think beyond sitting in the chair answering questions about your book.

Good Luck! If you make it to air, send me an email with what you did. Even send a link where I can watch the segment. You might end up in my next book!!!
jan@foxtalks.com

Part Five

You – The Bundle of Nerves

RINGGGGG RINGGGGG

You've piqued their interest and you get the call. You get invited to the studio.

Now what? You will know exactly what to do when you get there, if you follow these simple Fox Talks tips - some things to think about before you take your seat under the lights.

And the Gavel Comes Down Hard

1... 2...3...4...5...6...7...8...9...10

10 SECONDS!!! That's about how long you have to make a great impression in your TV interview. Thumbs weigh heavily on the remote control, so your look, your voice tone, the first words out of your mouth are getting the Judge Judy once over from the get-go.

That's why so many people fear speaking in public, let alone appearing on TV. You know you are being judged. Tell the truth. You do it, too. You are watching and listening to someone speak and are asking:

- Credentials – does the person really know enough to tell me this?
- Voice – can I listen to this for 6 minutes or am I bored already?
- Presence – does the person have any? Is he/she engaging?

- Hair color – can I really learn anything from someone with gray hair, spiky hair, no hair?
- WIIFM – what's in it for me? Is the person really speaking to me or just spouting on about him or herself?
- Am I going to get something I can use here?

It is no wonder that most people, when they think about having to give a presentation or speak on TV, want to pull their hair out!

Fear List – Flops Test

Try this Fear and Loathing of Public Speaking test. It applies to your TV spot, because you will be speaking to thousands of people. Why will you be nervous? Check off the ones that apply:

- ☐ Embarrassing yourself
- ☐ Forgetting what to say
- ☐ Appearing foolish
- ☐ Boring the audience
- ☐ Not knowing what to do
- ☐ Sitting out there alone with an unknown interviewer
- ☐ Sounding stupid
- ☐ Being challenged

Fox Talks-Flop Test Results

If you checked:

0-2 - You just need a few small tweaks. Keep reading.

3-6 - Keep reading and do all the Practice Plan Pages in this book for 5 minutes, twice a day.

6-9 - Keep reading. Do all the Practice Plan Pages every chance you get and call Fox Talks for coaching ☺.

Your Choice:
Baton Twirling or Affirmations

I have often helped shy guys turn into good speakers. I simply showed them how to twirl a baton or made them do the Cha Cha with me.

I gave them a baton and showed them how to do the under arm twirl. After a lot of uproarious laughter from the group, there was the VP of a company twirling. Yep! There was a former Army Sergeant and professor at West Point doing the under leg pass.

I can't say the Purdue Golden Girl had anything to worry about!

But why did I do this?

I always explain to the group that when they are asked to speak or be on TV, they are asked for a reason. You should feel ridiculous if you are asked to do something you don't know. You should worry if you are being asked to make a fool of yourself. That is not the case when you are called to be the expert. I tell the poor baton twirler:

"Look. You are the VP or the Army Sergeant. You know something that not one other person in the room knows. You are the expert. The rest of the people in the room are here because they want to hear you. All you need to do is just stand and share what you know. I could be asking you to twirl the baton."

After the laughter subsides, the shy speakers are loosened up. They get the point. They are ready to go to work. They are ready to own what they know. I sometimes ask them to put their arms out like a bear hug toward the audience. The concept of "Embracing the Audience" can help the speaker imagine himself / herself as just one of the group, not the person set apart at the front of the room.

Sometimes even good speakers get those same jitters when they have to go on TV for the first time. I tell them I have a baton for them, if they don't kick it in gear to work on the nerves. Funny how they feel better about the TV segment after the thought of baton twirling!

Jan's Platitudes

The truth is, you need to just think of yourself as if you are just talking to a good friend. Remember, this producer needs you. You are a conversation starter sharing your life's work and mission. In any other place, you love to talk about this topic. It should be no different for you under the lights.

My list of platitudes can also cure fear. You've heard them before, so you simply have to practice believing them. Say them every day until studio day.

- You are a gift. No one else can deliver the content you own.
- You are the expert.
- You own the credentials.
- You are the invited guest for a reason.
- You have what the audience wants to hear.
- You are fully prepared.
- You are obligated by the universe to share what you have.

People need you. You are a giver.

When the nerves start closing in on your throat and your mind, just start repeating this list of affirmations in your mind. Start believing. Ask yourself this question: Can anyone else do what you do the way you do it?

You know the answer is NO, so own it. Bring it!

Jan's Comfortability Continuum

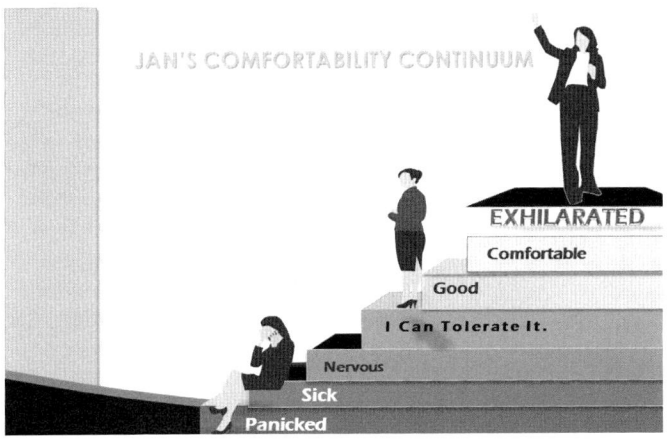

For all you teachers and grammarians out there, I KNOW "comfortabilty" is not a word. I made it up to combine your comfort level and your own feelings about your ability level, when it comes to speaking in front of people and, worse yet, the thought of doing it on TV.

So where are you?

Panicked? Sick? Nervous? I can tolerate it?

Good? Comfortable? Exhilarated?

If you are on the left, panic may set in. Maybe even real panic attacks. One woman told me she had to get drunk or, at least, have a drink, before going on.

OH, NOOOOO! That's real fright and a very bad idea. Especially with all the Judge Judys watching.

Then there's the one who's sick and gets nauseous, just can't stand it on the purely physical level. Many can tolerate it and know they can get the job done.

Moving on up the continuum are some who say, "Oh, I feel quite comfortable with this. I've had some good evaluations in the past."

Finally, some of you absolutely get exhilarated.

That's the ideal.

What Audience?

I worked with a CEO who had to give an annual meeting speech that was being videod. He did a really great job. He shared personal stories about wanting to quit, but told how he pushed on to build the company to the biggest of its kind in the lower 48 states. At the end, his employees stood in long lines to tell him how great it was.

So I asked him how it felt – how he felt he did. "Pretty good," he says. "Everybody says I did great."

But when I asked him if he felt like the audience was with him, and if he could draw on their energy, he said, "Hmmmm, I didn't pay too much attention to the audience."

Oh, my! That's the whole point: to play off the audience, to be ONE with them, to ride the laughter, and love it. The really good speakers get to that level of exhilaration. That's what you want with that TV host – an instant connection. You want to get to exhilaration because that will bring a level of extra energy and engagement that the home audience can feel as you share your important message.

Some TV shows actually have a studio audience. You will want to BE ONE with that audience, as soon as you can make it happen. You want them to laugh at the right places. You want them to be nodding with you, when the camera pans the audience for the cutaway shots.

If you can adjust to the lights and the hustle and bustle of a studio, you will play that host like a sweet fiddle. You will draw your own energy from the interchange of the interview and the reactions of the audience. You will go with the flow. Trust that. If this level of exhilaration has served you well in the past, it will serve you under the lights.

Your Continuum Spot Again?

Wherever you placed yourself on that continuum, do whatever you can to just TWEAK yourself a little further to the right before you get to the studio.

A tweak is a MICROact that results in MAXimum Potential.

MICROact for MACRO Impact.

For example, you can almost tolerate speaking. Can you get to the "good" point quicker? Can you max out your passion? Or take it up a notch? Can you increase your energy level? Can you make eye contact with the host or the studio audience just a little longer?

Those are all Speak Tweaks. Here are a few more:

- Stop saying UMM. (more on HOW later)
- Add a short personal story. (more on that)
- Ask the host a question in response to his/her question.
- Let your hands do their thing as in any conversation you have with a friend. (More later)

These are small Tweaks.

See? You don't need a major overhaul to be a better interviewee. Take yourself where you are and practice a few of the Tweaks in this book. You will be amazed at how MICROacts can deliver bigger punch under the lights.

Just keep moving yourself toward exhilaration, a TWEAK at a time and DON'T GET DRUNK!

The *3 P* Pill

To make your mark in your segment and to get invited back, there is one big pill you have to swallow. It's called: PLANPREPAREPRACTICE.

I ran all the words together, because pills always have long names you can't pronounce. This one has 3 simple components:

- PLAN
- PREPARE
- PRACTICE

This is a pill you must take every single solitary time you get invited to be on TV or have to make a presentation. This may sound just as elementary as your teacher in 3rd grade saying, "Please do your homework." That's just what it is.

Key Word Sheets

I coach my media and speaking clients to use what I call, KEY WORD SHEETS, for practice.

You know your topic. You know the points you want to make. You live your material, so why write it all out?

BUT, you need to order it a certain way for a 7 minute segment, another way for a 5 minute segment, and so on. It takes careful and generous slicing and dicing to carve your life's work into a cohesive message you can deliver in a short period of time.

List the topics you want to cover. Write out some phrases for each. Take time to craft a few lines that you want to be sure to say a certain way, but not the whole speech.

Practice that list for a while. Finally, make a KEY WORD SHEET. It might look like this:

DRUNK STAT
JOANIE STORY
MOM
FOUNDATION
HELP for BILL
DONATE

For a short TV segment, these words could fit on a 3x5 card. Make several of them. Put one in your pocket or bag each day. You can pull it out anywhere to practice.

Put on the dash board or passenger seat of your car.

How about putting one on the kitchen counter and another on your bed side table?

Practice what you want to say for each point. As you look at your Key Word Sheet, don't always start at the top. Most speakers do that, so they are great at the opening of the segment or one of their speeches. They get shaky in the middle, and ad lib the all-important ending. They spend all their time practicing the top and run out of time in their short practice bursts before they get to the end.

Start at different points each time. You can memorize your opening and closing lines. Know those cold. Especially, get any calls-to-action "in the can", as we say in TV.

Key Word Practice Plan

Key Word Sheets allow you to have a cue, but talk more freely. You will be able to engage more with your listeners, ad lib with confidence, rest assured that your listeners will get the important points you want to make.

Use this system for other meetings or presentations every chance you get before your big TV day.

Key Word Sheet Practice Plan

1. Make a quick Key Word Sheet for your next business meeting. Try following it as you talk.
2. On your next phone call, even to the kids or a friend, jot a quick Key Word Sheet and see if you can follow it.
3. When you are delivering a report, lose all the notes, just work from a Key Word Sheet. Are you still as smooth? Do you feel more room for engagement?

And the 3 P Pill? You don't get to take it just once. You have to take it every time you speak in front of other people, and, for sure, when you make your first TV appearance.

If you are a hit on your debut, you will get invited to speak somewhere, or you may be asked to come back to the show. That's the good news. It just means you have to take this pill again and again and again.

Don't leave anything to chance for your big day.

Part Six

You – The Determinator

Jan's Retainability Rungs

Your TV segment can do one of two things for the viewers – help in some way, or put them to sleep. The purpose you choose for your segment may make your audience snore. Let's see where your purpose fits on: Jan's Retainability Rungs

I know "retainability" is not a word, but how much of a chance do you give your audience to retain your information? The purpose of your segment may determine what the viewers will remember.

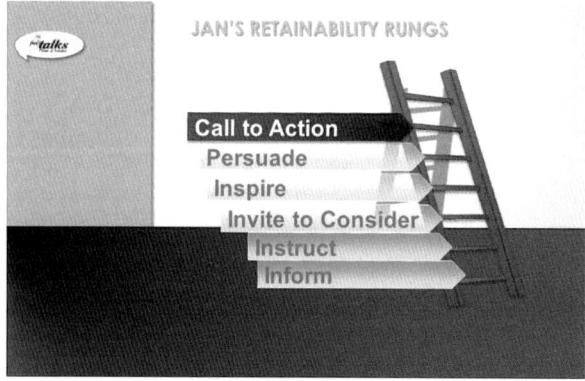

To Inform:

IF you are just trying to inform the audience with facts and figures, researchers say that the percentage of your viewers that will retain your information is only in the single digits.

Even if the group is mathematically inclined, if they only see the numbers, they will most likely forget them. If you use colorful language or personal stories to describe the information, a few more will retain the information.

If you turn the information from this:

> Increases to $7.25 on July 24th
> Tipped employees – must make at least new min wage (with gratuities included)
> If your min. wage is over $7.25 this change does not apply to you
> Go to www.laborlawcenter.com/t-State-Minimum-Wage-Rates.aspx to see if your state is included in this change

To this:

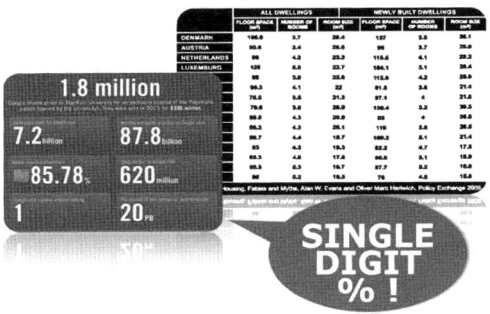

A few more people in the audience will remember it. Still, simply to inform is the bottom rung of retainability. it's hard to move an audience with bare facts.

To Instruct:

If you are instructing the audience – telling them how to cook, or how to do an exercise – they realize there will be a payoff for them, so they may keep watching. But, as a former teacher, I can tell you this: very few people have a learning style that allows them to remember information, if you just tell them. Your job is to show as much as you can. Take props or anything that will help you show.

If the viewers have tuned in because they want to learn what you have to instruct, your retainability factor goes up, but it is still only one rung up from just informing your audience.

To Invite to Consider:

We have iPhones and calls and tweets and texts and newsletters – many of which we don't want. How long has it been since you were sitting at your desk, or you were listening to someone speak, and you had an aha moment? A real epiphany?

Those moments don't happen very often.

So when you invite people to consider something, it better be something that's going to change their thinking. It has to be thought provoking. It has to have the possibility that the light bulb will go off over their heads. This will take you up a rung. If they look up to hear you better. That is a huge step up the rungs.

To Inspire:

This is where your viewers really start to remember and, more importantly, ACT on what you are saying. One of the definitions of inspire is "...to influence or impel." Inspiring has the potential to move viewers off a dime. That's what every coach, trainer, or consultant wants to see.

FACT from lots of research:

The fastest way to change behavior is not through the head. It's through the heart! You've heard it said: "Reason drives decision making, but emotion drives action."

Studies show, that the reasons people change their behavior are not the rationales they get from their parents, or their bosses, or the great cosmic boss they may follow in their lives. They change because of what? An emotion:

> FEAR   LOVE   ANGER

Think about it. You change your actions when you're afraid. You change when you're angry. You change when you're in love or when you are excited. In some of my speaker coaching work, I ask the clients to scrub their content, only leaving in lines that will draw an emotional reaction from the audience. That's an art. In a 7 minute segment, it's a real test! The trick is to appeal to emotions in as many ways as you can in your interview.

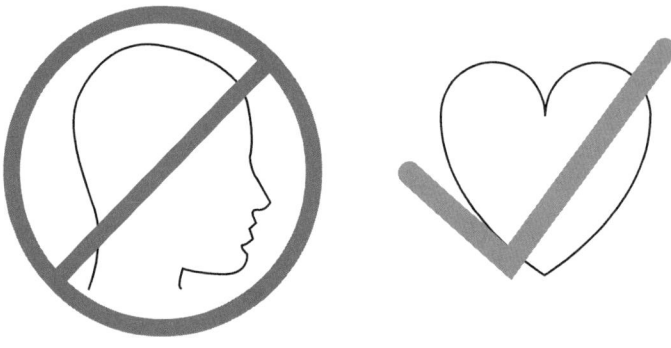

Even if it's a more technical topic, find a story to tell that leaves the viewers feeling. You have to make them feel something. You can't just let them go out with their heads full. That information will be gone soon. Send them out feeling. Then you'll get the action that you want.

Who can watch the small children in the ads for donations to poor countries without wanting to give? Your topic may not have that kind of impact, but give careful thought to what you want them to feel. Your answers to the interviewer have to give them reason to feel.

To Persuade:

You would say Martin Luther King inspired us. Right?

He inspired a nation long before some of you were born. He went a retainability rung higher. He persuaded us to act.

When you want to persuade your viewers, they have to know where you want them to start, POINT A, and where you want them to end up, POINT B. Vague persuasion doesn't move anybody. They need to feel specific pain to see the specific gain.

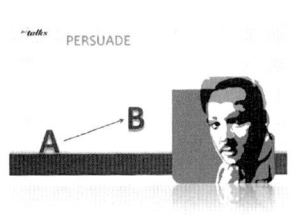

Describe Point A, and then what they will get at Point B. Arriving at a specific Point B is the only way to measure whether or not you've been successful in your persuasion.

You actually want them to feel uncomfortable enough at Point A to want to move. It's hard for the viewers to take the first step until you help them see Point B.

MLK showed us that at Point A, we were unfair and that some of us were hurting in our nation.

He then described Point B – a nation where we were all equal and where we all had the privilege of voting and going to any school.

Then he told us what to do – how to act – to get to Point B.

"Don't sit on the back of the bus. Don't fight back, if the police use brutality. Sit down until they hear us."

When you can give the viewers that kind of clear picture after you have inspired them, then they know where to start. You have persuaded them to move, so persuasion takes you higher up the ladder.

FOOTNOTE:

Lots of times the great interviewees will hit all of these rungs. Somebody in the viewing audience can remember best by taking instruction. Somebody can remember best by an invitation. Some need to consider. The more of these that you include in your segment, the stronger the impression you will make.

To Call to Action:

This is where you get the viewers to buy your product, to sign on the dotted line, or to agree to something. A call to action is where you really have to turn it on. Turn on every power of persuasion. Use every inspirational tool. Give them all the information you can find inside yourself. Paint every possible picture that will appeal to their emotions.

They step forward. They sign. You make the sale. You've then made it to the top of the Retainability Rungs. Your audience won't forget your message. They bought it and bought in.

Lots of Combo – Humor

Now it gets tricky. Do you ever want to try humor in your presentations? Are you thinking about trying to be funny under the TV lights?

Here's what happens: the true entertainers on TV are on Comedy Central or on late night talk shows. They have one big advantage: they have big staffs of writers.

One of the funniest guys I ever heard was a sportscaster on local TV. He had the best one-liners, when he was talking to the anchors, or describing sports scenes. He was as quick-witted as anyone I have known. It all looked so natural.

I watched him one afternoon. He sat at his desk in his sports office, carving out the very words he would use in that impromptu gag he was going to do on the show that night. He made it look so off-the-cuff, but he took the 3 P Pill. He planned, prepared, and practiced. It's an art form to be funny.

Let me try to demonstrate what happens with most people who try to be funny. I'm a grandmother so I get to do a granddaughter story. It's my right!

I'm with my granddaughter. She doesn't have one of those little tiny girl voices. She has a deeper, resonant, more adult voice. So we're sitting at a little no-name restaurant and she says: *"I kinda like that combo over at the Chick-Fil-A."*

I say, *"And what is a combo?"*

She says, *"A sandwich and a drink."*

"But what's in the sandwich?"

"Lots of combo," she says, with no small measure of indignation that I didn't know what a combo sandwich was.

Everybody in the little restaurant heard her disdain for my ignorance. They all roared with laughter.

When I am telling the story, if I deliver her funny line, in the same flat tone of voice as I tell the first part of the story, it gets lost. Most people even do worse!! They look at their shoes and lower their voice on the punch line! Why? They aren't sure it's funny and don't want to take the chance by laying it out there with gusto. So they literally put their heads down and swallow the punch line.

They are right. That swallowed line isn't funny and doesn't get the laugh. They don't deliver the line in a way that invites you to laugh. They shyly eat it as we look at the top of their head. That's what happens when most of us, who are not trained, try to use humor.

I'm saying to go for it on your funny lines, every chance you get. If you know you're funny, and people laugh at you most of the time, then say the punch line much louder than the rest of the story. Use the right facial expression and wait for the laughter, or at least, the snicker.

The idea is to make sure that you are inviting them to laugh. Ever notice how some of the talk show guys start clapping first after they say a funny line?

On the sitcoms, they put in canned laughter to force you to think it's funny.

Bottom funny lines:

- If you are going to attempt humor, try it out on many people first.
- Don't be shy on the punch line. Belt it out.

- Give the host time to react.
- Nod and laugh at yourself a little.
- Never try it, if you have any doubt about whether or not it's funny. It probably isn't.

Storytime

All up and down your retainability rungs, your most memorable moments will be your stories – no matter which purpose and rung you choose. TV does not lend itself to long drawn out stories, so use pared down versions you can tell in just a few sentences. Leave out all the dates, times, and set-up details that don't matter. Make sure every line you use has the potential to influence an emotion! Make every line make them feel. Use a

sentence to set the stage, another one or two to tell what happened. Then offer your life or business tip you draw from the story.

Quick, but still heartfelt. That's the formula you want. That said, where do you find good stories to illustrate your points?

Your own experiences are at the top of that list.

- Embarrassing moments
- Failures
- Successes
- Epiphanies
- Life changing actions you took
- Foolishness that turned out to work

If you are selling something, use your customer stories. The viewers can identify with the customer. This Fox Talks Business Story Outline will help you get the rhythm of shorter storytelling – still with a punch.

Business Story Outline

One of the fastest turnarounds I ever saw was in _____ ,

back in _____ .

The place looked like (vivid description)
_____
_____ .

It was also _____
_____ .

We had to just go back to the basics:
_____
_____
_____
_____ .

The first sign of a turn-around was (specific)
_____
_____
_____ .

So in (time frame) _____
_____ .

We had a ($$$$ amount swing) _____
_____ .

The (Clients, agencies, constituents, newspapers) said, "
_____
_____
_____ ."

Huge thrill or accomplishment because
_____
_____
_____ .

Don't ever use a famous person's often told story or quote on TV. You will be boring, e.g., if you tell Barack Obama's story of his humble beginnings to show how far he's come. B-O-R-I-N-G! Everybody already knows the ending. (That was NOT a political statement, just an example of something everyone knows.)

Tell about your own difficult beginnings, and then talk about the fact that where your path starts doesn't matter.

Storytelling is a true art. Doug Stevenson, Steve Denning, Annette Simmons all have books on the subject. Read them – or one of them – before you try a story on a TV audience.

It will be worth it, because stories will be what your audience will remember most. You won't forget what's in a combo sandwich, will you?

Stories connect, relate, motivate, communicate, and reach us on that emotional level in a way that just facts and figures never can.

Phenomenological Experience

One very high level story-telling technique can generate a "phenomenological" experience for your audience. That's exactly what you want.

What it means is that, as you tell your story, you have to feel it deep in your soul and heart, as if you were living it all over again. You simply let your own emotions from that original moment show as you tell the story.

When you feel a specific emotion, your audience will feel it, too. The deeper you feel it, the deeper they will feel it.

Just why do you want them to feel your feelings?

Every time you speak or appear on TV, you are trying to give the audience something to help them move from one point in their lives to a better point.

If they feel the pain you were in as you describe your situation, they will feel the need to follow your feelings to the relief, euphoria, or pride that you feel as you succeeded in moving yourself to the better point in your own life.

You are offering pure hope. You are handing your viewers possibility. One speaker I know says that is the best gift you can give anyone!

In order to give it, you need to create that phenomenological moment. I just say, "You need to tell your story so skillfully in such a heartfelt way, that you make the feelings in the pit of your belly jump in the bellies of your audience." Then they will jump to the edge of possibility.

Isn't that an exciting personal / professional opportunity?!!

In a business sense it means they will buy your product, donate to your cause, try your idea, buy your book.

Isn't that why you wanted to be on TV in the first place?

(This can be a whole day workshop. Call me!)

Notes:

Part Seven

You – The Stylist

The Big Day...
Before You Leave Your Closet

Think simplicity when you dress. You don't want me to ask, "What the heck is she wearing?" or "Where did he ever get that tie?." Big flowery patterns and big color block designs detract from your message.

No Muu Muu

I had a funny moment as a talk show host – to the staff behind the scenes – not to the guest. A woman, who wore a big blue muu muu with bright colored flowers to a TV interview, got it caught on the arm of a canvas-backed captain's chair.

As she got ready to exit the set, she took a few steps and the chair yanked her back. She scraped it across the set, yelped, stopped and looked back and couldn't see anything, so she yanked, scraped and yelped again – several times.

I had to keep talking to tease the next segment. I could see her in my peripheral vision, but had to look that camera dead in the eye and keep talking - AND WITH A STRAIGHT FACE!

I could see the technician behind the camera doubled over in laughter. The woman finally wriggled it free, but my message is don't wear a big muu muu to the studio.

You want what you wear to be no fuss, no muss, no drama, no danger!!!

You want the viewers looking at your mouth and eyes, not at your wardrobe.

No Jewel Chest

You want the viewers to be able to hear you, not distracted by clanking jewels. I was coaching a woman not long ago, who had two big Pandora dangling bracelets on each arm. I could just hear the distractions when they rattled around and banged on the microphone. She wasn't too happy when I suggested she not wear them.

They were presents from her children. I told her that if she wanted her children to hear what she said when they saw her on TV, she would leave them at home.

Big baubley necklaces run the risk of banging on the microphone, too. It's a nasty noise that will interrupt the interview.

You also want people to be looking at your face, not drawn down to your chest by a string of big beads.

Men and Zig Zaggie

Gents, if you wear one of those herringbone shirts, or a tie with teeny tiny checks, TV cameras will make them have zig zaggy shadowy lines that move and wiggle. Very distracting.

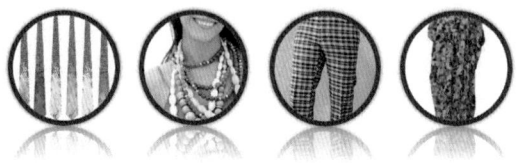

Big, bold, wacky ties make us think you were wacky for wearing it. Of course, you may want us to think that, so go for it, if it is part of your schtick.

Rule of Thumb

Look at how the host and others dress for the show. If you see suits, pull out the suit. If they roll up their sleeves like Anderson Cooper, keep it casual.

Hair Raising

The hottest hair styles may look trendy in real life but more like the proverbial egg beater on your head in front of the camera. Women anchors used to wear the traditional anchor helmet. Think Jane Pauley and Andrea Mitchell.

The producers and make-up/hair stylists wanted neat back then. You have eons more flexibility now, but you still don't want me and other viewers to ask, "What planet is her hairdresser from?" Or do you? Sometimes a look is part of the gig.

My own daughter took a job as the traffic reporter on a competing TV station, from where I was working in town.

She has a LOT of long curly reddish hair. The manager of the Traffic Office asked the TV General Manager if she should cut her hair.

The GM said emphatically, "Oh, NO! She is known as 'the girl with the hair'. A moniker of any kind is great!" So if you have something that stands out on purpose, go for it!

And, Gents, you may not know this, but women don't dig those big comb-over dos. And whoever told men they look great in that reddish hair dye that seems to dye blotches on their pates?

Natural is better.

Shallow?

Don't be so shallow, you say, but you know the first thing you do when you see something out of the norm on a TV person, is make fun of it. Right there, as the viewer is doing that when you are talking, you lost your first point. Don't let that happen to you, when you are in the spotlight.

Sometimes, it might be good to design a quick throwaway line to make sure your viewers get their first judgments out of the way. Something like: "The.......... is such an important topic. Thanks for the chance to discuss it." Then your viewers may have settled back in to listening mode, if something you wore distracted them.

Mirror Check

Look in the mirror in your TV get-up. Where do your eyes land first? That's where your viewers' eyes will land. Is that where you want them? If not, back to the closet.

Does the color of it light up your skin and eyes, or does it dull you out? Is it flattering to your shape? Does it add to the level of professionalism you are trying to achieve? If not, start over.

Makeup Matter

Make yourself up the way you normally would. Thicker, brighter, smoother is what you want to go for, because HDTV shows every line – even lines you didn't know you had. Most local TV shows have eliminated the expense of the legendary makeup person. You can always get a free makeover by stopping at a makeup counter in a department store. If you can afford the expense, a professional makeup person may make a huge difference in how much you like the look of yourself in the replay. Sometimes, it's worth every penny.

Big make-up mistakes:

1. The orange line that goes around your chin, where your make-up stops. Take it on down your neck. Blend better than ever.
2. Too much eye goop, so people can't see the sparkle and passion in your eyes, as you speak. It works for Lady Gaga, but not for you, if you want a serious response to your TV segment.
3. Men, lose your pride. Use a little matte powder to pat lightly on your forehead – especially if you are just plain bald in front. That always glares under the lights, so matte pat it down. Ask for matte powder that matches your skin at any makeup counter.
4. Left-over makeup on your collar or dropped down the front of you. Be careful as you apply.

Part Eight

You – The Prep Fanatic

Points with the Producer

TV producers often think they are the most important people in the world. They run the show from top to bottom. They are too busy to get back to you or too hassled to be as specific as you would like. They are used to barking orders, just once, hoping the receiver gets them.

Try to ask the producer or booker these questions: Talk fast. They are generally not listeners. They are doers. Have these questions ready when they call or email to book you.

- How much time will I have?
- How would you describe your viewing audience?
- What questions or topics might come up?
- Would you like any additional questions from me?
- Will any other speaker be involved in the segment?
- Will there be a rebuttal after me?
- Where do I send my photos, props, or DVDs, etc.?

Friend to Your Viewers

Do your homework. Know your interviewer – your new best friend. You'll learn by watching over and over. Know your intended audience intimately.

- Who are they?
- What do they do?
- How old?
- Likes and dislikes?

What will make them want to watch you, listen to you, and STAY with you until your message is complete?

Google the TV show. Find out who watches, what the demographics are. Know as much as you can before you go.

Watch the host or anchor often until your big day. You will have a good sense of the flow and pace you will face.

Stop Watch

You have mounds of material you can talk about easily.

Cull just the key points, the triggers that will cause a viewer to do something to help your cause. Then work your message into the allotted time frame. Time yourself with practice interviews several times to make sure you are in the ball park.

Smart phones have stop watches. Time your answers. 10-15 second sound bites get repeated!

Longer, drawn out answers get forgotten – or worse – interrupted.

Know the points you want to make ... cold – You want your answers to have 4 Rs:
- **Relatable,**
- **Retainable,**
- **Repeatable,**
- **Returnable**
    – as in good enough to get you invited back.

Part Nine

You – The Performance Consultant

Voice Appeal

You have your at-home voice, your yell-at-the-wife voice, your growl-at-your-husband voice, your workplace voice, your interview voice, your in-front-of-the-boss voice. Decide the tone of your message before you ever hit the studio.

PRACTICE IT! Take the morning paper. Pick a story. Be yourself, but read it out loud as if you were speaking it to someone. Keep reading until you find the tone you want to use. Make sure it is your most authentic voice that makes you feel comfortable. Then practice it with your material.

Flat Line

The last thing you want, after working so hard to get on TV, is to put us to sleep. Nothing does it like a monotone voice. Most of us think of that as a flat line. "Blah blah blah blah" – all in the same tone of voice. It can be high, low, loud, soft. If it is a flat line, nothing will help it.

But if you listen very carefully, ANY pattern that keeps repeating, can turn into monotone.

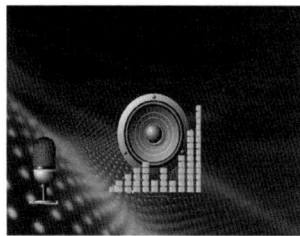 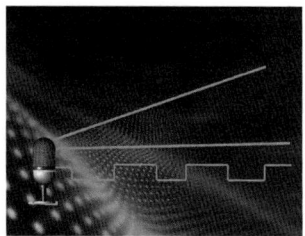

When you raise your voice up and talk about something, then you go down and talk a little about something, then you raise it up and talk about something, then you go down and talk a little about something – that pattern gets tiring and turns into a flat line of its own.

All Important

If you generally speak with an adamant voice, as if every line is important, nobody knows what really IS important.

The only variation in voice tone of the "ALL IMPORTANT" speaker is the short breath in between each line. This is tiring to the listeners. They tune you out. You leave them missing your most important points. They can't figure out what they were.

Excite-O-Meter

How much genuine excitement do you usually bring to your topic when you are speaking about it? How much excitement are you using when you usually speak about your product or topic? How much are you using when someone buys your idea? That's what you want for TV, but there is one big factor: TV lights and mics flatten you out, so you have to take it up a notch on your excite-o-meter.

You need to add extra energy when you really want your viewers to get interested in a particular point. Your iPhone makes it easy for you to practice. You will see the flattening I'm talking about here. What can you do to raise your excitement level? As a reporter, I had to increase my natural volume or I looked and sounded flat.

Slow Boat to China or Lightning Bolt

Now let's take a hard look at Pace.

Ask anybody who knows me and they will tell you that I have a tendency to be a Chatty Cathy doll. Just pull the string. The more excited I am, the faster I go. Can you imagine a lightning bolt?

There are several problems with a lightning bolt speaker:

- Talking too much!
- Adding a bunch of points together, so some get missed.
- Getting to the monotonous,

flatline zone by going too fast.
- Sounding like a thoughtless airhead.

On the other hand, when did you ever hear a talk show host or a news anchor who sounded like he/she was on a slow boat to China? Almost never. That means the slow speaking guest will drive the Type A host or anchor nuts! Simply put.

Varying your pace helps create interest in the listener's ears. Go fast when it's a fun, upbeat point, or when you want to make it seem urgent.

Slow down, if you want us to think about something a little longer.

You can use any of these variations at the appropriate time, but not in any pattern.

Voice Type

Do you know your voice type?

- Betty Boop – the high pitched, squeaky little girl sound coming out of a powerful looking woman. That is always off putting.
- Ted Knight – the old fashioned, deep throated, fake anchorman style – from the Old Mary Tyler Moore Show - oops! just dated myself. Doesn't sound real.
- Mousy – sounds unsure and timid and won't impress dominant hosts or viewers.

- Ooh la la girl – won't get you far with strong female hosts.
- Arrogant Arty - sounds like you know it all. Most people are turned off by this type.

I once interviewed the late John Kenneth Galbraith – a famous economist in his time. Right before the interview started, as Arrogant Arty, he asked, "How much time do we have to do this?"

"About 7 minutes," I answer.

"Hmmmph! Frankly, my dear, that's just enough time to make my whole life's work seem totally inconsequential."

I was rocked, as a new host. But I will tell you, that voice is embedded as a bad, bad memory in my mind. When I hear that arrogance in a TV guest today, you can hear the "click" of my remote from here (MD) to Kansas!

Record yourself. If you don't like your voice, a coach can help. Get it fixed before your big day. Sometimes, it's just a couple of tweaks. That way, you won't worry about how you are going to sound. You will know. You'll own your message when it's time to give it.

Think of yourself as your most robust, powerful, persuasive self.

That's the voice that's right for you.

Passion! Think Passion!

Practice, as that robust self, giving your answers as if you were in love with your words or your topic. Your passion should be contagious.

When you feel it, your audience will take it in.

I coached Dr. Judson Brewer, a Medical Director at an Addiction Clinic at Yale. He was asked to give a TEDx talk that would be recorded. I don't think he will mind my saying this, but he came to me sounding fairly academic. He ended up on that stage having pure fun as he talked. His passion was palpable. Within two weeks, he had 50,000 views, now well more than 100,000!!!

Check it out. When you feel his fun, you will know what I mean.

http://www.youtube.com/watch?v=jE1j5Om7g0U

You won't need to take notes with you to the studio. You are the expert. Just speak the info you know and practiced with your Key Word Sheets, the way you practiced it. Listen to the interviewer and just respond naturally.

Audience Wiifm

Remember, you are going to be in the viewers' bedrooms, their kitchens, their comfy family rooms. Ask yourself: What's in it for them?

They want to believe...

- that you have confidence in what you're selling or talking about
- that you have incredible willingness to help them at any cost
- that you have empathy for their issue
- that you'll give every effort - work around the clock for their cause
- that you are more intelligent than they are, so they can trust you

Let your voice tone, patterns, posture help the content give them all of that.

You have heard many times, "Just be yourself." I'm just suggesting that you practice being your BEST self.

Umm Um Uh Err Er

If you are an "umm um uh err er" speaker, you really need to break that annoying verbal pause habit.

Why? Researchers say "umming" your way through a speech, a presentation, an interview, or even everyday conversation makes the listener think:

- You are less intelligent than you really are.
- You don't know what you are talking about.
- You are not prepared.

You don't want any of those misperceptions out there, so here's my simple technique for fixing it:

SHUT YOUR MOUTH!!!! That's right – shut it!

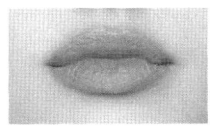

You've seen Angelina Jolie on the front of all the magazine covers, haven't you? Remember those lips? They're almost always lightly closed with that faint smile.

An "um" or "er" can't slip out, if your mouth is closed.

Umm Umm Practice Plan

Here's a five minute a day practice plan to break the habit, once and for all:

Pretend someone asked you a question – right now.

Got it?

SHUT your mouth before you start to answer.
Say a few words out loud to answer.
SHUT your mouth to think. Then finish
your sentence.

Let's try that again.

Answer this question out loud right now:

What was the last thing you thought about before you fell asleep last night?

- STOP!!
- SHUT your mouth. Think first.
- Start to answer.
- SHUT your mouth. Stop to think.
- Finish your answer. SHUT your mouth.

This takes a lot of practice, if you are a chronic "Ummer". Start today. Driving in your car. Cooking dinner. Watching TV. Talking to friends and family. Practice talking without those "UM's".

This will make your "listenability" go straight up.

Those "umms" actually cause tiny stalls in your listener's or viewer's ability to hear you. Every time you do one, the listener has to get back on track. That doesn't do you any favors. It means they may lose or miss some of your most important points.

Hands Down

A big question is: What to do with your hands? Answer: Just about what you always do with them when you are talking.

Just as you have a Voice Type, you also have a gesture type:

- Chicken wings – This is where your elbows go up and down and do all the work, instead of your hands. Looks disjointed.

- Conductor – This is where you are pointing to imaginary places.
- Waver – A hand that kind of waves back and forth is like hypnosis to the viewers.
- Pointer – This can look aggressive.
- Sleepers – They just lie in your lap and do nothing.
- Innies – This is where your hands are always cupped and sort of pointing back to your chest. Is that really where you want your viewers to be looking? This actually makes you look shy and powerless – even exclusive.
- Outies – This is where they just splay out to nowhere.

If you are a big person, and your gestures are teeny, it looks disjointed. If you are a small person with really big gestures, you can look slightly wacked! Like you are trying too hard to be bold.

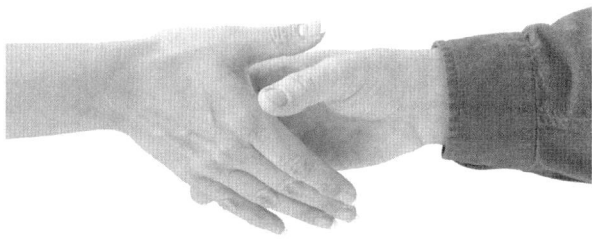

Stop and shake hands with somebody right now. As you unfold your hand to take it away, STOP!

That slightly unfolded hand is the perfect gesture. You can point with it. You can use it to connect to the host. Think "inclusive". That's what you want your hands to be saying.

Your hands just need to follow your words. If you are talking about something big, spread them out. If you say the word, "everywhere," do a little sweeping gesture with them. If you are saying something in an adamant tone, small chops are ok. If you are saying, "You can understand that.", gesture to the person. Let your hands go where your words go. Let your hands help your audience visualize your message

Hands Practice Plan

Here's another practice plan. This one for your hands:

- Shake hands with 3 people. Make that extra skin between your thumb and fore finger hit theirs.
- As your hands are clasped, slightly start to unfold your fingers. That hand is now in the perfect power position for making gestures.
- Practice putting your hand in that ever-so-slightly cupped position – never rigid. Feel the power!
- Talk to your friends and co-workers with this gesture. Feel the power every time.
- Pay attention to what your hands naturally do. Try to envision how that works sitting in a chair on a TV set or standing at the demo table.
- If you are showing size or excitement, extend your arms way out. Bigger on the demo set is better, so everyone can see.
- Practice feeling inclusive – with your hands!
- With every conversation you have, let your hands follow your words.

Body – Voice – Words

An often quoted and mis-quoted study from a few decades back says, that our likability as a speaker or an audiences' ability to listen to us is based on:

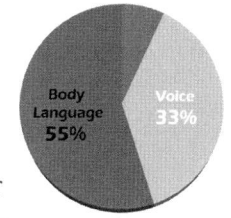

55% body language!!!
38% voice tone!!
7% – only 7% on word choice.

But where do we spend all of our time preparing for a talk or a TV appearance? On our words!!

If we only prepare WHAT we are going to say, we can lose a lot of our audience. Be prepared with your whole body.

One More Granddaughter Story About Body Language (A Little Politically Incorrect)

When my granddaughter was almost 3, she knew all about body language already. We were at a big family birthday party for the grandkids in Maine.

I decided to show how smart Kaden was and asked her a few questions about Cinderella. She was on a roll and then I asked what Cinderella said when she couldn't go to the ball.

Kaden made a mad face, crossed her arms, pushed

them down hard on her chest, twice, and then said in a loud voice, "D*mnit!"

When all the laughing stopped, I asked where she heard that word.

"My Daddy!"

"Whew!" I said. "At least, it came from the other side of the family."

But the little rascal proved a body language point. Her face and her crossed arms told us what Cinderella thought about not being able to go the ball BEFORE she said a word. She could have said, "RATS!, SUGARPOPS!", or "Oh, no." The word didn't matter. We already knew the feeling behind the answer.

You may not have to stand in front of a mirror to practice your body language.

Some speakers and TV guests do. I don't, but I try to envision myself in front of an audience making gestures that match the words that are coming out of my mouth.

I am no introvert, (understatement) so my gestures are big and bold – sometimes even tom-boyish.

My gestures would look ridiculous on an elegantly dressed, refined woman. I often call on such a woman in my audiences, ask her to stand and then ask the group if she would look right with my gestures. The answer is always – NO!

She would have to find what feels right for her.

I do believe we can all stretch our comfort zones to become the biggest, best presence we can be.

You have to find your body language comfort zone. One fast way to do that is video yourself with your phone as you practice a speech. Look at it. If you don't like what you see, or how you feel, keep the videos coming until you do. It could be 55% of your likeability factor.

Because of that, never, ever, ever stand behind the big brown box. That is death by lecturn!!

The "podium" is the riser you stand on.

Visual Rhythm

Your word choice and what you say set up an Auditory Rhythm for your viewers or audience to follow. They settle into it. Even if it has unpredictable moments, which is ideal, where you yell or smack your hands or whisper, your viewers get used to your unpredictable rhythm and like it. They watch for it.

Your guest spot on TV or any speech you are giving also has what I call a "Visual Rhythm". Your body language provides the visual rhythm. This, too, needs to be unpredictable, but never too unsettling.

Your visual rhythm should augment your auditory rhythm. It helps your viewers understand your message more quickly. It aids them in securing that ever important "retainability" you want to give them.

If you are on a stage or standing at the TV demo table, your visual rhythm needs to bigger, broader, more sweeping than when you are sitting in a chair on the set or presenting while seated at a big conference table.

Your gestures are like mini punctuation marks. You can't read a story without them. Your viewers or your audience can't understand your message as well without them.

Everything your body does on the stage or the TV set is just as important, or more so, than the words you say. The viewers will remember what they SAW before they will remember what you say.

Practice your Visual Rhythm as much as you practice your words. Video yourself. If you don't like what you see, CTRL ALT DEL and start over. Your viewers will thank you.

More importantly, they will hear your message more deeply making it easier to apply it to their lives. Isn't that what every speaker wants?!

The Chair

You can even practice the way you sit. Try out the couch

Try out the couch at home, stools, easy chairs at a table. Make sure you feel comfortable in all of them. You don't know what you will face at a studio or in front of a reporter.

When you watch the show you're going to be on, check out the chairs on the set. How many different sets or chairs do they use? Practice in all the kinds of chairs that you see on the TV show, to be sure.

Too much leg? Lazy-looking posture? Billowy or too tight clothes for sitting in a chair?

Men, does your jacket ride up your back and stick up at your neck? Remember the movie, Network News? The anchor man always pulled down the tail of his jacket and sat on it to keep it from riding up. It works! Is it better buttoned or un-buttoned?

Have somebody tape you with a flip cam. Study it. What do like about what you see? That's it! Remember what you like and duplicate it at the studio.

Posture, Please

Most chairs and couches cause you to slump and lean you backwards. You want to stick your butt as far back in the seat as you can, and then lean a little toward the interviewer.

No matter what the back of the chair does to you, you want to sit with a nice straight back, leaning slightly forward to engage, and still look and feel comfortable.

Part Ten

You – The Perfect Guest

Your Grand Entrance

Arrive plenty early. Get used to the noise, the constant chatter, the pace, the bustle. Newsrooms, especially, can sound and look crazy!

If they stick you in the proverbial green room, it's a relatively quiet place to gather your thoughts. But don't hesitate to ask them if you can sit in the studio until it's your turn. It will help you see and get accustomed to what you will be facing.

If you get to go in, act at home, as if you have been there before now.

Make it feel like home as fast as you can.

No Entourage, No Coffee

They hate it when you bring an entourage. Newsrooms are notorious for not having enough chairs. You aren't a superstar – yet! If you have a publicist, a manager, then one person may accompany you, but you need to be in charge of what you say and do.

Unless you are desperate, refuse their coffee! It tastes like it has been sitting in old pots for a long time. It has. And it's made so stiff, it can walk to wake up the morning dead on the early shifts. It will add to any nervous tension you have. Then you just have to figure out how to get rid of the cup of stuff you can't drink. I've seen coffee cups stashed behind plants and curtains! That's how bad it is.

I probably don't have to say this, but NO GUM! Ditch any mints or other lozenges before you are introduced to the staff.

Looking For...

The producer walks into the green room and calls your name. Those dreaded nerves kick in.

What do people always tell you to do before you have to make a presentation? Take a deep breath fill your lungs. That's true for TV, too.

I once hired a guy to do an annual meeting closing speech. The CEO is introducing this speaker. This CEO is as sophisticated as it gets – the BMW convertible, the creased trousers, tall, suave, quietly brilliant, highly influential in his industry.

Picture him at the podium:

"And now we're in for a real treat. We have John Smith with us today."

I swear! The speaker is in the back corner of the room– facing the corner – waving his long, skinny arms up and down fast, like a giant bird. He's breathing in and out in real short bursts. I am like freaking out. "Doesn't he know that the boss is saying his name? What is he doing?"

He had his routine. He simply had his own routine of doing his deep breaths his way. Then he ran to the stage with boundless energy. He sure woke us up.

Not many of us can pull that off, but you do need your own routine for calming your nerves.

Personal Power Points

I have discovered what I call, "Your Personal Power Points."

They are on your body, not on the screen.

You have to stand up to try this.

Stand on the balls of your feet. You will probably stand on the pad on the inside of the ball of your foot, right behind your big toe. You wouldn't usually stand across the whole width of the ball. Try standing on the whole width.

Now take a little tiny bit of an athletic stance – not the whole golf swing thing, just a little flex in the knees. The top part of you is standing up straight, but not rigid. Try to feel the exact connection between the ball of your foot and the floor. You can flatten your foot, but your weight is still in that ball.

So take a breath from down somewhere under the floor. Don't laugh here, but imagine that breath is coming from the center of the earth, up through your feet. Let it pass through your thighs, tush, belly and on up through your lungs.

As you exhale, say your name in the breath of your exhale. I bet you ten bucks that your voice went deeper, sounded fuller, and had more power, than if you just used your normal breath.

Try it again a few times. All of a sudden, when you hear that deeper, fuller voice, you feel more powerful. It has a rich resonance.

I have done this with hundreds of people in a room. They giggle at first, but after they do it, they all nod that they feel some new power surge! One guy even said he found a neck!!

I was coaching a VP of a very respected company in his industry. It was just to be a better speaker, not a TV star. The gent almost had to be pried away from the wall. His face - faced his shoes. I called him my, "shoe drooler".

Within a few minutes, I was able to get him to just lift his body a bit. Take that crazy breath a few times. Stand a little taller and lift his chin. He found a new posture - his own personal power point.

At the end of the hour, he walked down the hall - up straight - shouting, "Look! I have a neck!" Of course, a buddy said, "That's just your double chin!"

We laughed, but later in the day, he told me that the session and his new posture were like therapy! Now he is speaking at all of his industry meetings. He is the leader on a monthly all staff call, with his big voice, his no "um um umming", and his humor.

The CEO says, " Speaker Coaching changed the culture of our company. We sound and look like leaders. Now our people follow." All of that and I didn't have to use the words, "self-confidence", "self-esteem", "face your fear", one time.

I didn't do any heavy duty research on how to calm nerves or build confidence. And I certainly didn't do any emotional testing or study brain waves – all of which are incredibly important – just way out of my professional league. I simply straightened him up a bit, so his power had room to reside in his body. I think it was waiting right under his chin!

Use your personal power points and new power surge with every step from the green room to the studio, and your nerves will subside.

Remember, you are the expert, there to share what you know inside and out. They want to hear you! AND, you have planned, prepared, and practiced. You took the anti-nerves pill.

Once you sit down, you can make sure you're planted in that chair and you can still feel that deep connection in your feet to the floor. Take your deep breath from there. Let it out and own all of your personal power.

Notes:

Part Eleven

You – The Host Tamer

The Interviewer

Yakker – Quitter – Ignorer – Interrupter - Primper

Know your interviewer.

The **YAKKERS** love to hear themselves talk. I think most interviewers fall into this category. They introduce you, but then in the way they ask the first question, they also answer it and then keep talking.

You are left with two options: Wait them out or interrupt. I always say wait them out until they take a breath. If you start with, "Yes, and....", you might get a word in edgewise.

The **QUITTERS** ask a question, look at you to listen to your answer, and then look down at their notes to find the next question. That space when they look down can leave you hanging. Be prepared to continue with good content, but don't just ramble. Try to remain thoughtful.

The **IGNORERS** make you wonder if you have done something wrong! They ask the question, and then look bored as you answer. Don't take them personally. Just buck up and do your very best work to keep talking with passion. You have to set the passion level with these interviewers. Make them match yours, instead of falling to their lower level.

The **INTERRUPTERS** listen to part of your answer and quickly throw in their opinions or another comment that proves they are smarter. These interviewers require you to practice the 15-20 second sound bite more than the others. Be prepared with short, pithy, clever, poignant answers. You might want to speed up your speaking pace without losing your train of thought.

The **PRIMPERS** are concerned about their appearance. You can't always see what they are doing as you watch TV. They have perfected the arts of hair tossing, fingernail picking, lipstick applying as you answer. They know when their camera's red light goes off which means your camera is on your closeup. They can primp.

Your job with a Primper is to stay your course without giving into the possible distractions. Pretend the top of their heads as they are looking down or their adams apple if they are looking up to toss hair, are your audience. Learn to love and relate to that audience even if you don't have direct contact with the interviewer's eyeballs.

In general, practice taking out all the unnecessary words or language in the way you speak or think about your topic. Practice what I call, "Quick Hear Speaking". Skip all your flowery, professorial language, long adverbial phrases and anything else that could make a viewer ask, "What did she say?" No jargon!

The great interviewers LOVE 15-20 second answers. Then they get to ask more questions or cover more topics. They honestly want the audience to get the most information possible. If you have a wordy message, even the good interviewers will interrupt you or talk right over you.

Answers that are too short will leave the interviewers lost for the next question. They hate a "Yes/no" answer worse than anything.

The best guests look like they are ad-libbing, but they ALWAYS have a few stock lines ready to throw in.

That great sportscaster I mentioned earlier, who was thought to be off- the-cuff hilarious, even practiced off-the-cuff looking gestures! You do the same.

Showtime! Producer's Job

Here's the good news. There's a long list of things you DON'T have to worry about when you get to the studio, so you can focus on the task at hand:

- Somebody else knows how to work all that equipment. Ignore it until you are told to look a certain way or do something specific.
- The control room knows when you have to be where. Someone will lead you. Wait patiently.
- Somebody will mic you up, put the microphone on you, and tell you how it works. Never touch it. You could be in a union shop where only the technicians can handle the studio equipment.
- The technicians will tell you where your camera is. Most stations now work with three cameras:
- One centered pointed at you and the guest. That's the wide shot camera that catches the two shot of both of you. Your camera is the one looking directly at you. One at an angle a little behind you is for the interviewer.

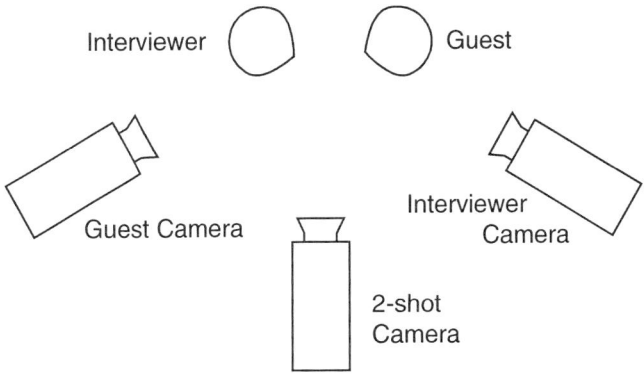

You need to know this going in, but once you are there, you don't need to worry about it. The professional camera people or robotic cameras will find you.

Note: When the interviewer is introducing you, he/she will most likely be looking at the center two shot camera. Just look at the interviewer as he/she starts to speak, but as he/she says your name, you can look out to the center camera, smile and nod a little, but your main job is to listen and engage with the interviewer.

Note 2: If you are standing up for a demonstration of some sort, you can always look at the central camera as you are doing something. The technician will tell you where to point your products to the close up camera.

Bottom line: know as much as you can about this going in and then don't worry about it when you get there. They will tell you.

- The host will set the pitch or volume. Just follow that volume lead. Match that volume, and you will

be perfect. If you think they lack a little passion, you can increase your volume.
- The host will set the pace. By now, you have watched them in action on your TV, so you know their pace. If you go a little faster or slower to get to your comfortable pace, that's ok, but don't slow the pace down, or they will interrupt you. Don't speed up or you will sound flighty. Match their pace, if you can, and still be yourself.

If they use a makeup person, allow them to do whatever they want to your face. It will definitely make you look better, especially now that HDTV shows every line and furrow you own.

The finished work of art may not feel natural to you, but trust that the artist knows what the lights will do to your skin.

Showtime! Your Job

And here's a list of some items you DO need to be aware of to be at your best:

- Have an opening line ready. "Thanks for having me here," or other inane things like that waste the hosts time. The host may say, "Thanks for coming in this morning."

    This is your chance for content. Try something more like, "My pleasure. This is such an important topic. We lost five teens to drunk driving just in the last two weeks." Give a fact to get things started.

- Always assume you are on live until told otherwise. Some nasty gaffs have made on TV and radio because the guest thought the mic was not on. The red light caught some big time professionals off guard, too. Some no longer have jobs! You are always ON.

- If you hear yourself start to ramble and don't know how to stop, just stop, or take a breath. Remember, the host loves to jump in. That will save you.

If your topic is controversial, have an answer for every possible trick or investigative question. This is very important. You need to practice these. Never repeat the negative words in the question. Go straight to the positive answer.

Nixon probably went to his grave wishing he had never said, "I am not a crook!" It got repeated over and over and over.

Example question: "Some have said your group has misused funds."

BAD example answer: "We have not misused our funds." That could come back to haunt you. That will be repeated: "The group leader said that they have not misused funds."

Good example answer: "Our controller has justified every expenditure and we are confident we are on the right track." When that gets repeated, that's what the audience will hear in a positive light.

- Fidgeting with your hands or a mic cord can be very distracting. NORMAL movement is what you want. Remember, you have practiced this…for life – being yourself.
- Sit still, but use your normal gestures. Rocking is for babies. Tapping is for dancers.
- Lean slightly forward. Sit up straight. Slouching on TV looks even worse than normal slouching when you see the re-play. It looks lazy or non-committal!

Angelina Jolie Eyes

A TV monitor may be in front of you or near you. Do everything you can to keep from looking at yourself on it. Somebody will tell you if something looks out of place.

Just look straight at your host. You want face-to-face mirroring eye contact. If you hold your chin up and look down at the interviewer's eyes, you look cocky. If you look up with your head down, you look shy. You want your faces to be on the same level.

Pretend you are Angelina Jolie. Those EYES!!!!!

Ever see her on the magazine covers at the checkout? Is she staring at you? Yes, with the most intense eye contact I have ever seen. No other celebrity can make eye contact like she does from a magazine cover.

I noticed it and then walked on to the cashier and looked back at her. She was still staring right at me.

And, yes, when I got to the end of the conveyer belt to get my bags, I took one quicker look. There they were – those piercing eyes still staring right at me.

Your eyes are your connection to your TV audience. Let your eyes help you speak!

Do not be a **HOVER CRAFT** – looking above your host's eyes. Whoever taught speakers to do that taught us to lose our audiences!!

Do not be a **SHOE DROOLER** – looking down at your feet to avoid SEEING your host or the studio audience.

Do not be a **LIGHT HEAD** – bouncing your eyes looking everywhere but at your host.

Think **BLACK DOTS**. I have learned that I make better connections of I try to stare or look at the black dots of someone else's eyes. That refines my focus.

An amazing thing happens when I focus on speakers' black dots. I remember more of what they say.

Just remember, you want to look 'em dead in the eye!

Practice Plan For Sincere Eye Contact

1. Tell your family members or a good friend that you need their help to practice good eye contact.
2. Start by just staring into the black dots of their eyes for 10 seconds. Really hard, isn't it?
3. Let them talk for 10 seconds while you look into their black dots. Then you talk and let them look at you. This is very hard to do.
4. Now increase the time to 15-20 seconds. Can you do it?
5. At your office or at dinner, force yourself to look into someone's eyes, at least for a couple sentences, as you start to speak.
6. If you look away, start again to speak, looking back straight into their eyes.
7. Try to draw energy from those eyes, and keep looking and talking.
8. Repeat this practice plan every chance you get for 21 days. You will not believe how your eye contact improves. You will be thrilled with the new depth of your connections.

Notes:

Part Twelve

You – The Two Timer

The Tease, as They Say in the Biz

See if you can think of an add-on topic, or another angle to your topic before you head to the studio. As the host is getting ready to wrap up and thank you, you can always say something like, "And maybe another time we can discuss...." Or, "And we do have a couple of other options ....".

You can be much more clever and conversational, if you have felt comfortable and have had a good time with your host.

"One other statistic will shock you but ... I guess I'll have to come back for that one." Wink. Wink.

Repeat Invite

Send a unique thank-you gift and note. Again, make it refer back to your topic. A box of brownies won't do as much as a chocolate replica of something in your topic.

Add another laminated sheet with a proposed follow up segment. Make sure the topic intro and questions are listed. Include spoon fed research, if needed, like a book with a quick outline prepared.

Keep it short and sweet.

Critique Time

No station or producer wants to hear you ask for a copy or dub of your segment – ESPECIALLY AFTER THE FACT. No one has time to look up the information and send the email.

Make sure you have at least two copies running at home or in the office or with a dubbing service, if you need hard copies or DVDs!

Tell them you need a link to your segment ahead of time. They can prepare for it.

Take a look at the copy of your segment. Look at it honestly. You will focus on what you don't like right away. Also, focus on what you did like. Congratulate yourself on those things and commit to repeating them next time. Write down what you liked and didn't. Then ask a colleague or friend to do the same. Do they match up?

It's a guarantee that you will be harder on yourself than anybody else. What do you need to do to improve? Can you see it for yourself? Start to practice it. You may get invited back. You want to be ready.

Pitch some ideas to other outlets and see if you can improve on your last appearance.

Producers have brought in many so-so guests. If you are upbeat, smooth, and clever with your content, you will end up on the circuit. I'll be watching.

On To The Networks

If you are stellar, and get invited back, collect and edit the best pieces together. Hire a professional to do it for you. Make it look as snappy as the promotions you saw on TV, advertising your upcoming segments.

You can send that link or DVD to PR agents or producers of network TV shows. Please do not send it, if you have any doubts as to whether or not it is network quality. You only get one chance to run your name by those producers. Make it worth their while.

And, if you want to make sure you are at your best, call me! I'll run you through your segment and coach you – tweak you – so you can show up with your fullest potential at play!

Break a leg, as they say. Don't forget, if you make it, send me your links. I'll write about you in the next book.

Notes:

Part Thirteen

Fox Talks Extras

100
Ideas to Get Yourself on TV

THINK PROPS! BRING PHOTOS! See how many follow up segments you can make up for some of these.

Some of them aren't new, but a new title, a new twist, an additional step can make them hit the re-fresh button. A Step System – 3 Steps to… - can simplify old messages for the viewers.

Financial Planner –

1. TAX TIME doesn't have to mean, "Oh, NOOOO!" 5 quick tips to survive the IRS
2. Retirement Worries? It's not too late to get better prepared. 7 Steps to …..
3. The Holidays Don't Have to Break the Bank. 3 tips to save fast…
4. 12 Days to Dig out from Under Holiday Debt

Eye Doctor –

5. Summer Fun means Special Eye Care. Are you prepared?
6. 5 Hot Tips for Trendy Sunglasses
7. The Right Glasses Shape for Your Face
8. Sunburn can mean dry eyes. 3 steps to prevent it.

Health Coach –

9. What goes on your holiday party plate if you want to keep off the weight?
10. Alcohol – How many calories do those two little drinks really add? 5 alternatives to overdoing it.
11. The latest science on how to lose weight
12. Supplements? What do I really need? How can I cut the cost?
13. Kids' Lunch Box – How to Healthy – ize it and have kids still eat it.

Cosmetic Doctor –

14. Latest trends – before and after
15. Tried and true – Tips to look your best at any age.
16. Lipo – 20 years later? Was it really safe?

17. Botox – 15 years later? Did it really help?
18. Summer – 6 summer skin care steps
19. Winter – Dry skin: 5 tips to prevent it. 5 tips to fix it.

World changer –

20. Small steps to make a Big Difference
21. Where are we needed most? 5 Ways to get involved where it can count.
22. 5 Projects that are working – Why and how do we help?

Entrepreneur coach –

23. Why small businesses fail - 5 Prevention steps
24. Build your list of clients right now!!!
25. Ways to save FAST before it's too late
26. Get a coach! 7 Reasons to get help
27. 7 Signs you know you need a coach
28. 7 Ways to Make Sure You Get the Right Coach for You
29. 7 Reasons your Coach is Not the Right One for You
30. 7 Ways to Get out of a Bad Coaching Situation

Real Estate Agent –

31. 5 Cheap Steps to Expensive Curb Appeal
32. Sellers' Market – What to Do to Make Big Gains
33. Buyers' Market - Deals to Steal
34. Trends and Tips

Interior Decorator –

35. Tips and Trends
36. 3 Seasonal Style Changes
37. 5 Quick Steps to a Big Makeover Look
38. 3 Easy Care Plants to Soften Your Style

Etiquette Trainer –

39. Get the kids ready for the family holiday dinner
40. Biggest Mistakes Adults Make

College Planner –

41. 5 Places to Find Unused College Money
42. 6 Ways to Cover Your Financial Bases
43. Tests to Find out What Your Kids Need to Get Ready for Maximum Learning

Fitness Coach / Physical Therapist –

44. 5 Quick Tips to Start ANYTHING
45. Walking Made Easier with Good Shoes – What to Look for When Buying
46. New tips for Running Safety
47. 7 Alternatives for Bad Knees and Back
48. Work out Your Neck Pain
49. When to See a Doctor

Hair Stylist – Make up Artist –

50. Hair Donation – Don't Just Cut It –Donate It
51. Easy Summer Styles
52. Win a Makeover
53. Grow Hair Faster with 5 Easy Steps

Therapists / Relationship Coaches –

54. Re-shape Your Morning Routine with Your Spouse – See Results Fast
55. Damage of Drinking too Much in Front of Children
56. Why Kids Need to Choose Their Own Clothes
57. When One Spouse Talks and the Other Just Nods – Now What?
58. 6 Tips for Getting on the Same Money Page
59. Handling the Switch Off- Kids and Divorce
60. The Fuel of Procrastination. Do you Recognize it? What to Do About It.
61. Gratitude – the Fix All - Add to the Credit Column
62. Flexibility – "It's who I am," is not an acceptable answer

Book Author – MAKE YOUR TITLE VISUAL – Put it in a basket – examples:

63. Cookies in the shape of some aspect of or word in the title
64. Basket of healthy snacks for health book
65. Basket of toddler clothes and snacks for Mom Book
66. Dollar bills turned into flowers or I-R-S letters for finance book
67. Newfangled small piece of fitness equipment for fitness book

Stress Management –

68. Photos of what stress does to your brain – Brain Sense!

69. Don't Just Tell Me to Breathe – Tell Me WHAT TO DO!!
70. 6 Steps to Manage Stress for Super Hyper Type A Personalities

Branding/Marketing Your Business –

71. Brand YourSELF, too.
72. Best Brands, Bad Brands that Went Away- Why?
73. Say it / Show it Like We NEED It
74. Solve My Problem – Are You MY Answer

Veterinarian –

75. Unusual House Pets
76. Treating Simple Problems at Home

Home Health Aid –

77. 5 Signs that It's Time
78. What I Do to Make Your Life Easier

Construction Contractor/ Renovator

79. How to REALLY Estimate the Cost
80. Top 10 Mistakes Homeowners Make
81. Easy Home Repairs - Series?
82. 5 Reasons to Stay Away from Do-It- Yourself Lighting Fixes
83. Constructing an Airtight Contract
84. 5 Signs of a Sure-Fire Rip Off

Social Media Expert –

85. Next New Time Grabber

86. 5 Ways to Tell Where You Should Spend Your Time (Stack pages to show- never try to do this live! Toooo slow!)

EVENTS PLANNER – Think EVERY HOLIDAY –

87. Fun Table Settings for 8 or 80
88. Decorations for any Budget
89. Fun Weddings on a Budget
90. Entertaining the Boss

CHEF – NUTRITIONIST – Think EVERY HOLIDAY –

91. New Year's EVE- Mini-Bites
92. New Year's DAY Leftovers
93. Easter / Spring - Traditional and/or New and Sassy Recipes
94. Memorial Day – Make it a Holiday for Kids
95. Fourth of July Picnic Pails – A Picnic "Basket" for Everyone
96. Summer Fun - Unusual Places to Visit
97. Thanksgiving – New Twist on the Old Bird or Why Have a Bird?
98. Kwanza – Colorful Table Spread
99. Jewish Holidays - Traditions in Beautiful Presentations
100. Christmas – Family Favorites with Flair

P.S. I could keep going, but I got to the end of the page. What can you dream up for your occupation?

Pitch Pattern

To Answer the Dreaded – "What Do You Do?"

You can always start with a question related to your topic: Do you ever get nervous when you have to speak in public, when you have to file your taxes, when you have to have a difficult conversation with your boss or husband or kid? Their answer sets up a problem that you can fix.

Q1. _____
_____

Q2. _____
_____

I WORK WITH (TYPES OF PEOPLE) _____
_____

TO (FIX, SOLVE, ANSWER _____
_____

their problem of _____
_____

by _____
_____ .

One of my clients, said, "_____ (great one liner testimonial) _____
_____
_____ ."

Q&A Is Not The Enemy

Once you have been on TV a time or two, you will undoubtedly start getting speaking requests. One of the biggest fears for speakers at live events is the Q&A period.

At your television segment, you gave the interviewer the questions. You knew that most interviewers are short on time. Maybe some are even a little lazy, so they will use your questions or similar versions.

At a live event, you never know what you're gonna get! No wonder that's a little nerve fraying. With some tongue in cheekiness, I guarantee that Q&A is not the enemy.

All you have to do is look backwards to believe you can handle it.

1. If you have negotiated a toy out of the hands of two screaming kids, you can negotiate an end to a long winded question.
2. If you have had to handle big or even small business deals with complications, you can get out of any complicated question.
3. If you have had to speak spontaneously anywhere and had a great feeling after it, you can trust yourself to do it again and again when you answer questions.
4. If your hubby or your wife happened to be rude to you and you deflected the tension, you can use that same skill and trust it with a rude questioner.
5. If you watch TV or listen to radio talk shows, the best answers are the 15 second sound bites, not the run-ons. Keep your answers short and move your eyes to the next hand or to another part of the

room as you finish your answer. This signifies to the questioner that his time is up and that you aren't interested in a follow up. If he/she insists, it's pretty easy to say, "Let's take some others and you and I can chat at the end."
6. Up close and personal contact with the questioner lets the rest of the participants listen in. They feel they've had an intimate moment with you, too. Q&A offers a priceless connections for referrals and future work.

Finally, Q&A shows your audience you are a master of fast thinking. You can also use your answers for humor opportunities. The laughter resides in your interchanges with the participants.

The chuckling is their personal memory stick. You just built in RETAINability and the possibility that the group will ask for you again.

I think the benefits of Q&A outweigh all the risks. You WILL get through a tough spot. Look how many you've wiggled out of in your lifetime already!!!

Of course, this is all dependent on your knowing your material cold and being able to say, "I'll look into that for you," when you don't know an answer.

Go for it!

*This article was published in the March 2013 issue of SPEAKER Magazine – the prestigious official publication of the National Speakers Association.

nsaspeaker-magazine.org/nsaspeaker/201303#pg1

Coaching/ Consulting Packages

Jan Fox's proprietary SPEAK TWEAKS Coaching System guarantees quick results. She says she rarely sees a client who needs a major overhaul, when a few tweaks will make a huge difference.

She finds that most people come to her bringing their most authentic selves. Most know their content. That means Jan uses her years of experience and considerable observation skills, to offer simple pointers and polishing, netting big results.

"Jan's speaker coaching changed the culture of our company. We speak like leaders. Now our people can follow."

– CEO, Peter Hill, Billy Casper Golf

"Our daughter improved 1000%!!! Your coaching works!!!"

– Father of Tori Nonoka, 16 year old National Pistol Shooting Champion

Story Fitting

One of Jan's claims to fame is what she calls, STORY FITTING.

One of her clients says, "Jan teaches us to speak the unspeakable." The tough stories – a child bride who suffered abuse and got away, a woman molested by her dad, women who had no voice, CEOs who failed, a woman with a program for Veterans too difficult to explain – these stories flow out of Jan's clients with ease.

She has a unique way of getting the tough stories out without emotion – one small memory or happening at a time. At the end, the client almost always feels immediate relief.

The child bride said, " I never told my story from beginning to end to anyone. It's out."

Jan uses key words and a few phrases for each small segment. Together, she and the client take out anything, details, that won't leave the audience feeling a deep emotion – line for line.

Then the "fitting" starts. Jan says, "Nine times out of 10, the pieces have a magical way of fitting themselves together. If not, we fit them piece by piece."

After the child bride told her story at a women's group to a rousing standing ovation, she was invited to give a TEDx Talk. Keep in mind, this was only the second time she EVER told her story. Take a look at Zarif Sahin. Make a hash mark, if you can remember, every time you feel an emotion as he tells her whole life story in 7 minutes!!!

www.youtube.com/watch?v=OHBaOyaltpU

Business Stories

Business stories are known for being dry and boring – full of facts. Jan helps sales teams, CEOs, entrepreneurs, and others who have to kill what they eat, take a fact and turn it into a personal result for one of their clients. When they tell those stories to potential clients, the sales are easier to close.

Research shows those sales people who know to use stories, metaphors, personal examples simply sell more.

At an all-day training session at a large IT firm that works on lucrative contracts for the federal goverment, a young but brilliant sales professional began his story attempt like this:

"Remember the Agony of Defeat?" The whole group laughed and started chatting about the skier that always falls off the jump. Dennis joined in the conversation like a pro, and then brought it back. " I was thinking, do you remember how all the old time skiers came down the jump with their toes together? They broke records, but then there was this guy who came down with his tips slightly apart so he could lean into his skis, a little more. Remember what happened?"

More chatter, then: "That's right, he went so far off the jump he landed at the feet at the people in the bleachers. The committee had to move the bleachers back. Of course, he shattered records."

Chatter- Chatter: "Yep, every skier does that today."

The whole group was nodding, while probably wondering where he was going with this.

"Well, I was wondering instead of thinking about this project as too big, even possibly insurmountable, if we could think of it as just spreading our tips a little. Look at the starting point and go on down the slope with our tips apart?" Heads nodded YES all around the room.

What are you feeling or thinking about that story right now? You might be asking yourself where you could spread your tips in your life, or your business? That can be a life changing question. Business stories don't get any more powerful than that.

Jan was invited back for quarterly training and coaching sessions.

Speech Prep

Getting ready for an important speech or presentation? That could be a daunting task especially, if it could lead you up the corporate ladder.

Jan gets you ready in record time, with a whole new level of "confidence" without ever having to say that word. Check the testimonial page.

She uses all the tips and tweaks in this book about how to act and what to do in the studio, to help you present your best self:

- Stop dreaded Umms and Errs.
- Create a powerful presence

- Improve Voice tone.
- Learn what to do with your hands.
- Leave your audience with "Golden Nuggets "of wisdom with high "retainabilty factor".
- Perfect the power of storytelling.
- Get comfortable working the room.
- Commit to deep eye contact.
- Learn when and how to use voice pace and volume to get attention.
- Develop compelling power point or other visual aid.

"Jan Fox is the best money I ever spent!"

– Chris Efessiou, CEO and Author of, *Chief Daddy Officer*

" Jan Fox is the best coach I ever had."

– Peabody Award and Emmy Winner – John Sherman, WBAL –TV

Media Coaching/ Training

You see 30 years of TV experience on the pages of this book. If you want help developing a segment, call Jan.

If you want help doing your very best job when you get to the studio, call Jan.

Jan's Speeches

Sharpen Your SPEAKability - Increase Your Impact

Jan's proprietary *"Sharpen Your SPEAKablity – Increase Your Impact"* program has helped law groups, PR firms, corporations, small business, sales and business development teams, associations, and women's groups raise the level of their communications and increase the confidence and influence of their employees.

"Jan was so helpful to our sales team, that we want her back on a quarterly basis. She built confidence very quickly."

– VP Agilex, one of the DC area's fastest growing IT companies.

- Speaking in public, but needing to cure knocking knees?
- Going on sales calls, but looking to power up your close?
- Presenting to your team, but wanting to persuade more effectively?
- Communicating lots of words, but wishing for better connections with the audience?
- Dreaming big, but believing you could deliver your vision with more passion?

This dynamic, interactive, action-packed SPEAK TWEAKS Program guarantees that you will walk out a more powerful and compelling speaker. Quick results!

- Learn one physical move that makes your new confidence almost palpable.
- Discover your personal power points – not on the

screen – on your body!
- Cure the "**uhms**", "**errrs**", and "**ahhs**" – your sure message blockers – once and for all.
- Figure out where your eyes should REALLY look. Angelina Jolie will show you, sort of, and you won't forget it.
- Work the room like a pro. Are you a Glue Stick, a Hider or a Bumble Bee? You'll see what you need to be to deliver with power.
- Lose the "I" out of your presentation and put in more "we".
- Stop "Stall Language" that keeps you from getting to your most important points.
- Make your hands a deliberate part of your presentation. Delete "Dreaded Hanger Disease".
- Fix what you don't like about your voice type. Do you know it?
- Avoid the voice "Flat line".
- Cure "Death by Podium".
- Understand Q&A is not the enemy.
- Put the POWER in your ppt.

"You are a miracle worker. I thought I could never speak. Even after you and I met on the Sunday , I didn't think I could do it!! Thank you with all my heart, I could NEVER have done this without you!"

– Laura D'All, VP Copy General

Speak Tweaks Hot Seat: Participants will have a chance to experience the "Speak Tweaks Hot Seat". Deliver lines from a presentation. Instant critiques.

*You will walk out with a FREE Minibuk of 5 Minute Speak Tweak practice plans you can do in your car or anywhere. Includes: 25 PowerPoint Points, Pitch Pattern, Business Story Outline.

"I have seen 100s, maybe 1000s of power points around the world. This is in the top 5%. Good. Really good. Original."

– Sam Horn, Best Selling Author of *POP!*

Power Of Tweaks:
MICRO Acts To MAXimize Potential

Jan believes in the Power of Tweaks – MICRO Acts to MAXimize your Potential. This dynamic, motivating, interactive keynote made a high level government official say, "Miss Fox, you set people free in here today. You set people FREE!"

- Can't find the starting point for the breakthrough you need?
- Feel overwhelmed a by the tasks looming ahead?
- Designed the big strategic plan but nothing is happening?
- Want to affect change but can't see the path?

Count how many breakthroughs you have had in your past. You have more in you. The quickest way to change is by small moves.

Three "R" Tweaks deliver fast action.

#1 RESILIENCE

- Become a champion of Plan B.
- Think ADAPT and ADJUST.
- Try mini-tests. Check. Try again.

We can draw from our vast reserve of Resilience to Unbury the next Breakthrough. You'll laugh at Jan's whistling "S" story.

#2 RESOURCEFULNESS

- Look for the next option.
- Jump at the next opportunity.
- Welcome the next challenge.

YOU ARE YOUR OWN BOSS! Work from the center of your own ethic.

This is how Jan made it from selling newspapers and stealing radishes in her small home town, all the way to reporting and anchoring in top TV markets. Even winning EMMYS!

#3 RESOLVE

- Lift an inch and walk boldly.
- Muster courage at every small turn.
- Master PURPOSEFULNESS.

Jan offers a compelling story that leaves you committed to fixing what's broken before it's too late.

Participants will walk out with:

- new sharpened focus to use the 3 "R"s at work and maybe in life
- deeper dedication to their purpose
- clearer path to their next breakthrough
- higher levels of engagement on the job

- greater productivity in less time
- more willingness to accept change

From participants' comments at a national conference in San Diego:

"Great enthusiasm and interaction. Engaging speaker. Instantly started to work on what she taught me. Friendly, humorous, informational. All the materials are great and followed along with the presentation. GREAT SLIDES. Everyone should attend this seminar. Empowering. Jan is the MVP of the week."

Get Yourself On TV & What To Do When You Get There

Jan's speech about Getting Yourself on TV is hysterical. When they least expect it, Jan pulls a live lobster out of a cooler to illustrate a point.

Do you have a great idea or business that more people need to know about, but just can't get any media attention?

Find out how to think INside the box to get INside the TV studio. Learn insider tips to make sure you get the producer's ear.

It's not about writing a better email or just sending your book in a press kit. The best way to a newsroom is in a box!

Hear how red velvet cup cakes, a box of live crabs, and a cookie bouquet netted the invite. Learn to think through your EYEballs.

You'll find out what NOT to wear under the lights, plus where to look, how long to talk, what to do with your hands, and how to actually manage the interviewer.

The frosting? Hear the guaranteed secret to getting invited back.

Every participant walks out with a Plan to Persuade the Producer and a Plan for Your Ready-Made Segment.

"I tried for 5 years to get on WUSA9 TV in DC. Within one month of meeting Jan Fox, I was a guest with JC Hayward."

– Omekongo Dibinga, International Activist and Author of *UPSTANDER*

"I had the honor of working with Jan to help advise me on a recent media spot. Not only was she spot on with her expertise, exceedingly generous and very supportive, but she also gave me some behind the scenes tips. The segment went so well that I was invited back for two more! You can't find anybody with greater enthusiam and warmth."

–Lois Barth, Acclaimed NYC Speaker, Motivational Expert

About The Author....

Jan Fox

Jan Fox's 4 EMMY AWARDS attest to her stellar 30 year career in local network news. But don't ask her where she went to Journalism School. The only woman role model on TV when Jan was a kid, was I LOVE LUCY.

She likes to say she came from a poor house in Shelbyville, Indiana, all the way to the White House and Hollywood interviewing many celebrities and US Presidents – a life she never could have imagined.

Jan spent a record almost 20 years as a reporter/anchor at WUSA TV9 in Washington, DC; 4 years as an award winning #1 anchor in Portland, ME; and 5 years as co-host of an Emmy Award winning talk show. Her "Sibilant S" start on that show was less than stellar. You'll have to hear the story.

Jan has been a sought-after "conversation starter" – her word for "speaker", facilitator, and emcee for more than 30 years. She loved the thrill of blowing the whistle to welcome a crowd of 16,000 to the Circus in Boston Garden.

She equally loves watching what she calls a "shoe drooler" stand up and speak with confidence. As a Speaker Coach, Jan has turned many struggling speakers into superstars on the stage. Her results are almost immediate.

No matter the size of the audience, Jan watches for the light bulbs to go off, the heads to nod, the signs that show lives, they are a changin'.

Her proprietary "Sharpen Your SPEAKablity – Increase Your Impact" program has helped law groups, PR firms, corporations, small business, sales and business development teams, associations, and women's groups raise the level of their communications and increase the confidence and influence of their employees.

Jan believes in the *Power of Tweaks – MICRO Acts to MAXimize your Potential*. This dynamic, motivating, interactive keynote made a high level government official say, "Miss Fox, you set people free in here today. You set people FREE!"

She is the author of G*et Yourself on TV & What to Do When You Get There*, a no-nonsense book of insider tips helping CEOs, small businesses, entrepreneurs, coaches and others land guest spots on local TV shows.

Her speech about Getting Yourself on TV is hysterical. When they least expect it, Jan pulls a live lobster out of a cooler to illustrate a point. Everybody walks out with a Persuade the Producer Plan, and a Ready-Made TV Segment.

TV is a far cry from her first jobs – sweeping out her uncle's shoe repair and taking over her brother's paper route, both in the 3rd grade! She has been a teacher and an associate professor.

Clients include: AGILEX, Marriott, Verizon, The Defense Logistics Agency, The Veterans Adminitration, The CIA, HUD, Well Point and Anthem Insurance Companies, NACE – Car Week, Robert H. School of Business at University of Maryland, Women's Power Conference and many more, plus a personal favorite, wait for it….. The International Association of Pet Cemetery and Crematoria Owners, even after she told them she only has goldfish.

Jan holds a Master's Degree in Education from Lesley University, where she eventually directed the Outreach Program.

She is a proud member of the esteemed National Speakers Association and was the DC Chapter 2012 Member of the Year.

Her list of COMMUNITY SERVICE AND MEDIA AWARDS is long and varied.

Jan says, "All this must not be bad for someone who has already retired TWICE!"

She lives just outside of DC in Maryland, with her hubby and those goldfish, but she spends as much time with her two grandkids as is grandmotherly possible.

"Your moving and passionate delivery riveted the audience's attention – men and women alike. You..improved lives that day."

– R .Adm. Sandra Stosz, Supt. U. S. Coast Guard Academy

Speak Tweaks – 5 Steps To Stellar Speaking & 5 Minute Practice Plans

To order copies of Jan's very popular minibuk,

foxtalks.com/products-page/

$5.00 FREE SHIPPING

Deeply discounted for group purchases or multiple copies. For more information, info@foxtalks.com

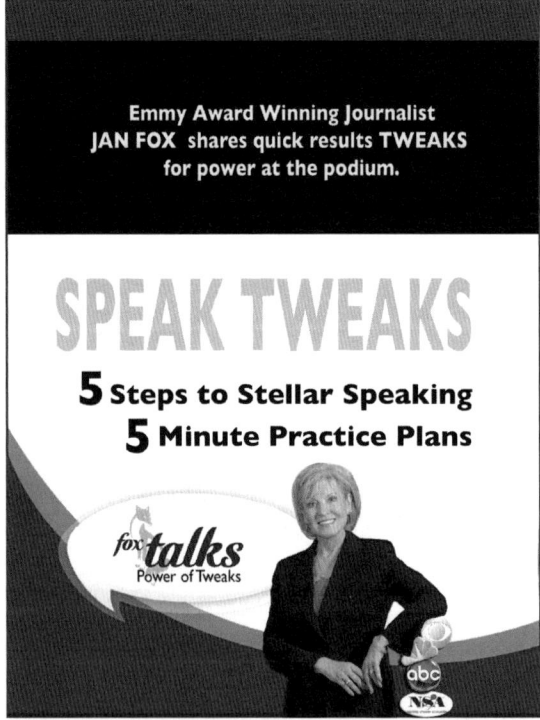

Image Credits

The below were used with Creative Commons licensing

Shoe silhouette – P. 11 – Mauricio Duque

http://www.snap2objects.com/

Backlava – P. 34 – Mumumio

http://www.flickr.com/photos/mumumio/

Scrap Metal Sculpture – P. 35 – 24oranges.nl

24oranges.nl